Recollections
of a GI War Bride

A Wiltshire Childhood

Sister Marie Elizabeth
with best wishes from
the author.

Margaret H Wharton

Dec. 1984

Recollections
of a GI War Bride

A Wiltshire Childhood

MARGARET H. WHARTON

ALAN SUTTON
1984

Alan Sutton Publishing Limited
Brunswick Road
Gloucester

First published 1984

British Library Cataloguing in Publication Data

Wharton, Margaret
    Recollections of a GI war bride.
    1. Marlborough (Wiltshire)—Social
    life and customs
    I. Title
    942.3'17   DA690.M46

    ISBN 0-86299-124-2

Typesetting and origination by
Alan Sutton Publishing Limited
Photoset Bembo 11/12
Printed in Great Britain

This book is dedicated to the memory of my parents

Joseph Frank and Hilda Sharpe Biggs

who loved and cherished me

FOREWORD

It gives me much pleasure to be asked to write a foreword to this book. Margaret Wharton is well qualified to write of this period in history, a story that needs to be told. It will be a valuable addition to the history of Marlborough and Wiltshire which has not previously been set down in writing, and posterity will be the richer for it. Margaret gives the 'feel' of Marlborough and Wiltshire, and so she should; her father was a great Wiltshireman, a real 'Moonraker', and she is a worthy successor.

J.E. CHANDLER

Chapter I

INTRODUCTION

Many years have passed from the time I exchanged the white chalk of the Wiltshire Downs for the red clay of the North Carolina Piedmont, going from Marlborough to Chapel Hill by way of Glen Rock, New Jersey. The road has not been tortuous or uphill – rather it has been a pleasant and rewarding passage through life. It has brought me personal happiness, professional success and now, at the last, time to reflect and summon up remembrance of things past.

At first it seems a far cry from a little known country town in the south of England to a small town in the American south. But wide as the differences are, certain similarities can be found. Both places are small, both are beautiful and both are centres of famous though very different educational establishments. Marlborough is very old but Chapel Hill is old too, on this country's standards. In fact, with its formal opening on 15 January 1795, the University of North Carolina at Chapel Hill is the oldest State University in the United States. This makes it older than Marlborough College, the renowned English public school, which first opened its doors to the sons of clergymen in 1843, though there is another less famous school in Marlborough which was founded by Edward VI in 1550. While Marlborough as a market town, centre of an agricultural district and home of certain rural industries, has always had a life of its own independent of the College and division between town and gown is quite marked, town and university seem to have merged and blended in the community of Chapel Hill. Perhaps this is the most marked difference in the character of the two towns.

It was my husband, David Wharton, a North Carolinian born, and just as proud to call himself a Tarheel, as I am to be a Moonraker, who selected Chapel Hill to be our home in retirement. After a working life spent in New York City, broken only by his five years of war service, he had a need and a desire to return to the state of his birth and the area where his pioneer ancestors had settled more than two hundred years ago. So on the threshold of our sixties, we left our New Jersey home of many years and made the trek south to Chapel Hill. Initially I was sick at heart, not for England, but for the home I had made for myself in America. But I have now come to realize that Chapel Hill will, in all likelihood, be our home for the rest of our days, and it is indeed a very pleasant place in which to spend them. Now my backward glances turn less often to Glen Rock but more to Marlborough, where in a spirit of gentle nostalgia, I seek to recall memories of my childhood.

The definitive point in my life was the move from England to America. For some years after my arrival in the States, I tended to think of myself as having two separate lives. The first began in England in 1917 and ended in 1946, when as it seemed, I was reborn in America to begin an entirely new existence. It was my work as a teacher – the career in education I pursued in both countries – that connected my two lives forming a bridge between them and brought me to realize how profoundly my life, both private and professional, was affected and moulded by my English upbringing.

It was the merest chance that led me to teach in America. One day over twenty-five years ago, my small son of five came home from kindergarten with a notice clutched in his grubby little hand. It announced a shortage of substitute teachers and a request that any interested and qualified mothers inquire at the Education Office of the local schools. I had trained as a teacher at Whitelands College in London and had taught in England for seven war-torn years. I had, I thought, closed the door forever on a teaching career when in 1946 I had arrived in the United States of America with my American husband. But with my two sons well established in school and finding myself faintly bored with suburban life, I responded to the challenge presented. And so began a long love affair wih the schools and children of the small community of Glen Rock, New Jersey, where I was to teach for almost twenty years.

After my initial visit to the superintendent of the local schools, I was told to apply for a Bergen County Substitute Certificate. For this my British credentials proved sufficient and in due course, I received a piece of paper that entitled me to replace a regular teacher for no more than twenty consecutive days. And then I waited . . . Perhaps the shortage of teachers was more imagined than real, perhaps my somewhat unorthodox training and experience made me a little less desirable than American trained teachers. It was many weeks before I was asked to take a fifth grade class for a Friday afternoon. I will admit to being nervous. How would my English accent, quite pronounced in those days, go over with the students? How about discipline? I knew from occasional visits to my son's classes that discipline was lax on British standards. Then too my training and experience had mostly been with older children and basically confined to English and History, naturally British. How would I relate to children in the elementary school? How would I cope with subjects such as Art, Music and Physical Education?

In spite of my fears that first afternoon flew by. My accent either charmed or hypnotized the children for I spoke and they listened. We covered the work left by their teacher in record time and my one and only gaffe came when I told the children to take out their poetry books. Not till then did I realize that an anthology of poetry is not standard textbook equipment in American schools. I quickly announced a book was not necessary and, thanking God for British memory training, recited 'The Pied Piper of Hamelin' to a spellbound class. My appetite for teaching was whetted and I had embarked on the resumption of my career.

My decision to teach in America marked the time when I began to think seriously about my English family background, my childhood and education and the two most important people in my young life – my parents. It was the time when the seeds for this book were sown, though I did not begin writing it for many years until I arrived in Chapel Hill in 1977.

Chapter II

I was born in 1917 in the ancient Wiltshire market town of Devizes, but it was in the smaller town of Marlborough some fourteen miles to the east where I spent my childhood and received my education from the age of five through to eighteen when I entered college.

At that time in England children entered school compulsorily on their fifth birthday – sometimes going earlier if space was available and the child appeared 'ready'. Each child stayed in the infants' school two or three years until reading, writing and arithmetic were well-established, when he or she was promoted to what was known in common parlance as the 'big' school. The school year was divided into three terms and promotions took place at each term's end. The infants' school was usually a self-contained entity with its own teaching headmistress, though it was often housed in the same building as the 'big' school. This latter school taught all children up to the age of eleven at which time the eleven plus examination was administered. The children who passed the examination went on to a secondary or 'grammar' school, while those who did not remained in their original school until the age of fourteen, which was the earliest legal school leaving age. The grammar school students took a school leaving examination at sixteen, while those who were college or university bound, stayed on till eighteen. It was this latter pattern that my own education followed.

It was in September of 1922 and some six weeks after my fifth birthday, that I began my school days in the forbidding grey stone building that housed Marlborough's Infants' School and St. Mary's Girls' School. St. Peter's, the corresponding boys' school, was at the opposite end of the town. Many years later, immediately prior to my departure for the United States, I was to do a short teaching stint in St. Peter's preparing eleven-year-old boys for the eleven plus examination. It remains one of the most interesting and rewarding of my teaching assignments. Each school was built in the shadow of its respective church in the pseudo-ecclesiastical style typical of schools hastily erected all over England to comply with the 1870 Act of Parliament, which made school attendance compulsory for all children.

I vividly remember climbing the steep stone steps, clinging hard to Mother's hand as she took me to school for the first time. I had some feelings of fear. My sister, almost two years older, did not like school and was having some difficulties. But the headmistress, a middle-aged lady named Miss Rowe, talked quietly to me before taking me into a crowded classroom to meet my teacher, Miss Collins. I took to school immediately but my days as an 'infant' scholar were short. Within a week I contracted scarlet fever and this, with complications, kept me in hospital and at home for six months. I returned but briefly to the infants' school, for being precocious, a good reader and very quick at figures, I was promoted to the 'big' school at the end of the year.

In the 1920s England was slowly recovering from the decimations of the First World War. Unemployment was high, many women were war widows left alone to raise children on minimal pensions, labour unrest was rife. Never again would society return to the pre-ordained and predictable levels of the Victorian and Edwardian eras.

The working classes, domestic servants high among them, and women had been liberated by the war. While men served in the trenches women had worked in the munition factories and had kept the home fires burning. Both sexes had proved their worth and realised a potential hitherto undreamed of. But all too often their new found freedom turned to Dead Sea fruit in the chaotic conditions following the war.

Such was the society in which I was reared and educated. I look back on my school years as happy ones that opened many doors. I was most fortunate in my teachers. One of the by-products of the war was a large number of young women robbed of their fiances or young husbands. Well educated, gentle people, they went into teaching as a means of making a living in a way acceptable to the standards of the society in which they had been raised. Poorly paid as they were, they gave to the children in their charge the love and discipline they would have given their own families had not fate so cruelly intervened.

I read of some who were embittered old maids, treating their classes with intolerance approaching sadism. But such was not my experience. We loved our teachers, respected them and learned from them. They taught us as much as they could and as much as we could absorb. I remember several ladies with love and gratitude. They were dedicated and committed women, teaching us manners and consideration for others along with reading and writing and arithmetic. They opened the worlds of nature, religion, history and literature to us.

Chapter III

Just as I was fortunate in my teachers, I was even more so in my parents. Locked into a poorly paying job, which he kept for the sake of security, my father, Joseph Frank Biggs, was a man of high intelligence and unusual talents and artistic abilities. Though his formal education ended at twelve, he had been the star pupil in the small Wiltshire village school of Alton Barnes. He was tutored and encouraged and treated almost as a family member by the impoverished but gifted village schoolmaster. At twelve, he was apprenticed in the barge building workshop at Honeystreet on the Kennet and Avon Canal, a business owned by his grandfather. Here he learned to use all manner of tools with great skill and to work with wood, a craft he developed to an unusual degree during his long life. But as canals were superseded by the railways, the barge building business fell on evil days and in the years before the war, the burgeoning auto industry beckoned him. After an apprenticeship in the Daimler works, he obtained a position as chauffeur to a wealthy squire, Alexander Grant-Meek, who owned estates at Manningford and Devizes. As a chauffeur, Father was responsible for driving and maintaining the cars and because trained men were in short supply, it was considered an excellent position. At the outbreak of the First World War, he volunteered for active duty but his service was brief because of a ruptured appendix, which almost claimed his life and incapacitated him for many months. Too debilitated for further military service, he returned to his private work in Devizes, where he maintained the family cars and drove them as long as petrol could be obtained. Then much against his will and his pride, he helped in the running of the estate, the staff short-handed because of the call-up of both men and women for war service.

In the early 1900s it was the custom for well-to-do local families to visit each other socially and during one of these peregrinations at the wheel of his Daimler, my father met my mother, Hilda Sharpe, a pretty girl who had started work at fourteen as a lady's maid and had become companion and secretary to a wealthy widow living at the Grange in the Wiltshire village of Worton. They fell in love and after a long engagement were married on 31 October 1911 in the village church of Erlestoke, where her widowed mother lived with several younger brothers and sisters.

My mother's family had moved from Herefordshire to Wiltshire where my grandfather had become bailiff and head gamekeeper at an estate, Erlestoke Park, bought by an industrial magnate named Watson Taylor. With their nine children of whom my mother was the eldest, they were living in prosperity, when a year after the move, tragedy struck in the form of appendicitis, in those days an inoperable and consequently fatal affliction. My grandfather died in his middle forties.

How often I heard my mother tell the story of how he was brought home from a shoot writhing in pain on a hurdle and how less than a week later he was carried out in his coffin to be buried in the churchyard at Great Cheverell. I wept as she told how his black

Labrador retriever 'Lady' lay outside his bedroom door, touching neither food nor water until, at last, the grieving dog had to be destroyed. All plans for the children's education had to be abandoned. My mother left school at fourteen and went into domestic service to contribute her pittance to the family income. My grandfather's employer, to his eternal credit, provided a small house and a smaller pension for the widow and children. There was a tiny insurance policy and somehow my grandmother, Harriet Lane Sharpe, held the family together in the face of poverty made more acute by its unexpectedness.

My parents began their married life in a small house in Bridewell Street, in Devizes. The street was named after the former prison which had once stood there, 'bridewell' being an old word for jail, a corruption of St. Bride's Well in London where a large prison was located. After my father's illness they moved to a larger house on Hillworth Road, close to Hillworth House, where my father worked. My sister, Frances May, was born in December 1915 and I arrived in August 1917. I was christened Margaret Hilda in the beautiful old Norman church of St. John – Hilda after my mother and Margaret presumably because my parents liked it. I was called Peggy from the beginning however and Margaret was reserved for official purposes and documents. By this time, my father's job was becoming untenable, largely because he was being pressured to do gardening, his pet aversion, albeit a strange one for an Englishman. He obtained employment in Marlborough driving for an auctioneer and the family moved there into a small row house in January 1918. The war was dragging on, victory was nowhere in sight, the Americans had not yet entered the war in force and there was talk of a massive German push coming in the spring. Influenza was epidemic, food shortages were critical, money was short, my mother was tied down with a fractious two-year-old and a five-month-old infant, my father committed to a job he never liked.

It was an unpromising beginning and yet over the years, we carved out a happy family life in Marlborough with my parents remaining there until their deaths in 1946 and 1964. I am ever grateful to them for the love and care they gave us and the values they instilled in us.

Chapter IV

My parents, especially my mother, talked to us about their own childhoods making us feel part of an ongoing and ever changing society.

Some years ago, my husband and I visited the small village of Lingen in Herefordshire, where my mother had gone to school. Memories of her tales of her childhood came flooding into my mind. She had told us about the plays the children used to put on in the village school under the direction of Mrs. Gisborne, the 'lady' of the manor and wife of my grandfather's employer. Mrs. Gisborne was responsible for the very elaborate costumes in the annual productions and I received a particularly detailed account of *Goody Two Shoes* in which Mother played the lead, and a vivid description of the blue satin panniered gown worn by little Bo-Peep. I never tired of hearing her tales. I cried when she spoke of her older sister's death. 'Edie' was the apple of her father's eye, a bright promising girl of ten when she fell victim to peritonitis, the result of a ruptured appendix. Search as we did in the overgrown churchyard that hot July afternoon, we never did succeed in finding her gravestone engraved with her name and the text 'Forever with the Lord' taken from her favourite hymn. But in the little church, entered through a lychgate and an avenue of roses, we did see wall tablets in memory of Gisborne family members and the choir stalls where some of the Sharpe family, my mother among them, had added their childish trebles to the swell of the Sunday music. In later years as my mother went about her household chores, she was prone to sing hymns at the top of her rather strident soprano voice. She had memorised the words, not just of the first verse but of entire hymns as a child in Lingen.

Mother had about two miles to walk to school and as the oldest child in the family after Edie's death, she was responsible for the younger children, sometimes carrying the smallest for long distances. The way lay along narrow lanes, muddy in winter but leafy and bedecked with flowers in spring and summer. The children used to pick the blossoms of the foxgloves and put them on their fingers. My sister and I were filled with envy for foxgloves do not grow in Wiltshire and we were also convinced that the Herefordshire bluebells and primroses were far more luxuriant then those of Wiltshire. In early spring, too, Mother, described fields yellow with wild daffodils, again absent from our meadows.

She also took charge of preparing the lunches which the children took to school and very often she would take extra food to share with some of her classmates for poverty was by no means uncommon in the agricultural districts. For the Sharpe family there was always plenty, rabbits, pheasants, partridge and venison from the estate – the gamekeeper's 'perks' – and vegetables and fruit galore from the big garden. My grandmother baked her own bread, made meat and fruit pies and all manner of cakes. She was an excellent cook, a characteristic inherited by all her daughters and one, I like to think, that has been handed down to me.

One of my grandfather's responsibilities was to raise pheasants for the great autumn shoots of the late Victorian days. The young pheasants were fed on dates and chopped hard boiled eggs and the older boys in the family were assigned this chore. Dogs, especially retrievers and spaniels, abounded in the house, my grandfather breeding them and training them for hunting. His favourite breed was the Labrador retriever and dogs of this type bred and schooled by him, acquired local fame. Cats were relegated to the outbuildings though one of mother's sisters used to dress kittens up, preferring them to dolls. Later my sister May was to do this when visiting this particular aunt. My mother must have had her fill of dogs and cats for she was not an animal lover. Only once did she weaken when my father brought home a tiny half-starved little terrier puppy. May and I were in ecstasy but our delight did not last long, for a few months later 'Mick' was killed by a car. Mother genuinely grieved for him and for us but the experiment was not repeated.

Mother spoke too of games such as draughts, backgammon and several varieties of card games played around the big kitchen table on winter evenings and of how the table was cleared immediately at any sign of altercation among the players. She told too, how her father waited in great anticipation for books sent from London – presumably his one intellectual extravagance. He was a great Dickens 'fan' and sometimes would go off into gales of laughter in his seat in the chimney corner. Sometimes, he would read choice passages aloud and then, willy-nilly, everyone listened. The kitchen was lighted by a large oil lamp and Mother remarked on the quality and purity of the white light which has never been duplicated. Our flickering yellow gaslight did not compare favourably. However, she noted the necessity for frequent cleaning of the lamp and how changing the fragile mantle was fraught with peril, as the lamp was a most valued and cherished possession – indeed, a necessity.

My grandmother was an authority on the Royal Family. She knew all the family ramifications, marriages and inter-marriages of Victoria's children with the crowned heads of Europe. She communicated this knowledge to my mother, an apt pupil, who in turn transmitted it to me. In my childhood, I made many royal family charts and trees under her expert guidance. Now as I watch 'Upstairs, Downstairs', 'Lillie', 'Edward VII' and other gems of British television, my knowledge comes back to me and makes the programmes more meaningful.

I learned too the dread of illnesses now preventable or readily curable. One of Mother's brothers had pneumonia nine times during childhood. As the eldest she helped her mother with the nursing and described the dramatic 'crisis' of the illness which came around the tenth day. She spoke of the epidemic diseases, whooping cough, diphtheria and measles – how dreaded they were and how all forces and energies were marshalled to cope with them. It was good nursing care that made the difference between life and death for little children, and all too often that was not enough.

My grandmother had ten children. Her best friend, Mrs. Redstone, the village schoolmaster's wife, had eleven. Though Mrs. Redstone lived in the village some miles away, they met at church, at school and village functions and whenever else they could. Pregnancy, of course, was not discussed in front of children yet my mother knew of the mutual distress whenever another baby was on the way in either family. The friends commiserated with each other and helped each other through the confinements. Mrs. Redstone always baked bread for Grandmother at such times and the Sharpe family did not like it as well as their own mother's. Some of the Sharpes' plenteous supply of food found its way to the Redstones' house where, bringing up a family on a schoolmaster's salary was difficult. It was Mrs. Redstone who noted that the earliest sign of pregnancy was turning against the morning tea. Tea, of course, was the mainstay and solace of English women. Mother herself said many times that as a child she thought life would be heaven without babies.

The highspots of my mother's childhood were visits to the local market towns of Kington and Leominster in Herefordshire and Presteigne, the county seat of Radnorshire. Thither she went with her father in a pony trap visiting the markets and shops. In Presteigne she tasted a banana for the first time, sampling peel and all and later describing it to her mother as a large yellow bean with a terrible taste.

Mother injured her foot at some time during her childhood. It became progressively worse until she was sent, at the suggestion of the village doctor and the manorial family of the village, to St. Thomas' Hospital in London. Though her foot was never quite normal, the trouble was arrested and cured. Her many week stay there, made a profound impression on her and her journey to London expanded her horizons beyond Lingen and Presteigne.

Chapter V

My father, who all his life was a great reader, was also a teller of tales par excellence. I can see him now sitting with a little girl on each knee, transporting us to the uttermost ends of the earth with his stories.

He also had a fine baritone voice and a repertoire of folk songs (no hymns for father!) and rarely a day passed that he did not regale us with a song or two. Oddly enough it is the American songs, 'My Old Kentucky Home', 'Swanee River' and 'Old Black Joe' that first and foremost bring my father to mind for the Stephen Foster ballads were great favourites of his. He had picked up an old violin at a sale – he claimed it was a very good one – cleaned and repaired it and he could scrape out a passable tune on it. He also had a flute which we loved to hear him play and a mouth organ in his pocket ready to be brought out at the drop of a hat. Years later, he made recorders and played them.

Father would also read aloud to us and recite poetry – his memory was prodigious and photographic. He was very fond of reading us *The Arabian Nights* and Greek mythology – his favourite versions in this category being Hawthorne's *Wonder Book* and *Tanglewood Tales*. As I grew older he introduced me to G.A. Henty's historical novels and Captain Marryat's seafaring adventures of which *Masterman Ready* was our mutual choice. He was careful to put the books he urged me to read in historical and geographical context and perspective. I also revelled in Robert Louis Stevenson, reading and re-reading *Treasure Island* and *Kidnapped*. *Travels with a Donkey*, required school reading, I found less appealing. I lost myself in Rider Haggard's African adventures – *She, King Solomon's Mines* and *Allan Quatermain* – but perhaps my favourite author at age ten or so was Conan Doyle. At Dad's suggestion I read *The White Company* and *Sir Nigel* for the first of many times. Both romances of the Hundred Years War, I once read *The White Company* (all 300 odd pages!) aloud to my patient mother – a project taking many weeks. She told me long afterwards that she knew it was important to me to share a story so thrilling to me with one who'd never read it. My mother always understood!

Oddly enough for a Conan Doyle enthusiast, Dad did not have much time for Sherlock Holmes. I think his tastes in reading inclined to the romantic and he did not have the analytical mind required for deductive criminology. He owned two bound volumes of *Strand Magazine,* about 1890 vintage, in which Doyle's *Adventures of Brigadier Gerard* had appeared serially. These I read and re-read thus gaining my first knowledge of the Napoleonic Wars. Also in the same volumes were a series of stories about a cavalry officer's adventures in the Indian army. Author now forgotten, I liked them very much and they started father off on tales of India, geography, history, myth and legend which I eagerly assimilated! I wish very much that I still possessed those old *Strand Magazines* but like many remembered treasures of my childhood, they disappeared after my father's death.

We also owned several volumes of *The Illustrated History of the Great War* and I spent a lot of time poring over the pictures and reading the captions while Dad added his graphic comments. Looking back, I realize the aftermath of the war coloured my childhood considerably.

Every Christmas was sure to bring me a copy of one of Father's favourite books. Some he acquired in a rather handsome leather bound edition. These I still possess. In his job Father went to many sales and sometimes for a few pence he would pick up boxes of books or toys. He had an unerring eye for good children's books, books which unless he could find them secondhand were beyond his means. One was a huge, beautifully illustrated edition of Andersen's Fairy Tales. Though Dad often read aloud from it, it was so beautiful that Mother would only allow us to look at it when we were ill in bed. On one such occasion, I disgraced myself by being sick on it. Mother, unexpectedly cross, said I could at least have pushed the book out of the way. Sometimes these boxes of books or toys contained unexpected treasures. In a box of old toys we found a miniature boat. Black with tarnish, a good polish revealed silver beautifully chased. Of antique Dutch origin, I have it still, standing among other silver ornaments on a small ornate table of my father's making. In a box of books we found a valuable edition of Shakespeare's *The Tempest* another item I salvaged and brought to America.

Father was also quite a student of nature. Many a Sunday afternoon, rain or shine, while Mother rested after her midday culinary efforts, he was delegated the duty of taking May and myself for a walk. We roamed Savernake Forest, the Kennett Valley, the high chalk downs. On those walks, we learned a multitude of things – the names of wildflowers, the names, habits and songs of all the birds we saw – we learned to recognize trees by their shapes, bark, leaves, flowers and fruit. We learned what plants grew in the high chalk uplands and which preferred the sheltered valleys or deep woods. We became aware of seasonal changes in plant and animal life. We learned why early man lived on the downs, open and exposed, with flint for their weapons running through the underlying chalk, and what evidence of this existence he left behind. Dad told us of the medieval feudal system and social development around the manor which gave rise to the villages. We learned to tell at which period a church had been built and to recognize any later additions. Father talked of ships and shoes and sealing wax, of cabbages and kings and I had willing ears and a receptive mind. Sometimes walking through the highways and byways around Marlborough he would tell us tales of far flung places. His own favourite reading consisted of travel books and he drew on them for his tales to us. Once his description of a wild boar hunt in Africa drew terrified screams from me when a frightened rabbit dashed across our path among the bracken in Savenake Forest. When I was very small, I often tired on these walks and remember returning home in triumph perched on Father's shoulder. While only slightly above average height, he was stockily and strongly built. He had well-marked features with a good profile and before he went bald had crisp curly brown hair. I thought him very handsome and loved him very much.

It is apparent, I hope, from what I have written that a feeling of belonging to a family was transmitted to us by our mother, while our father acquainted us with the world about us – its geography, history, literature, music and art.

My father's childhood was not very happy. He was brought up by his grandfather – just why was never made clear. His grandfather was a brilliant, though largely uneducated, man who had built a prosperous barge building business only to see it fall into desuetude through no fault of his own. He found solace for his business failure in drink. My father remained in touch with some of his cousins who had become quite successful. I think he was envious to some extent that they were more successful than he was. One had gone to Bermuda, I believe in a government capacity and visited us whenever his leave brought him to Wiltshire. Occasionally we visited an old man in Alton Barnes named Maurice Long. A beekeeper among other things, he was living in a big old house in something approaching squalor, but he had a fine aristocratic head and face framed in silver hair and beard. He was a great conversationalist and I gather he had been a surrogate father to Dad and there was great affection between them. But Mother never liked to visit him and I never learned much about him or my father's family.

Dad's best friend was Frank Butler, son of the village schoolmaster, and it was with Frank and his two sisters that my father experienced something of home life. Frank became quite successful as a timber merchant. They were present at each other's weddings. Though his visits were infrequent, he stayed in touch with us till his death. Again I fancy Dad was a little envious of his success.

Frank's two sisters, Mercy and Dolly, never married. They were teachers. They ran the village school at Mildenhall (pronounced Minal) just outside Marlborough when I was a child. We would occasionally walk the two miles to take tea with them in the tiny house attached to the school. It was built of grey stone and was in the shape of an octagon and headed with a miniature turret. I remember the thin bread and butter and homemade cakes and jam and the admonitions prior to arrival to mind our manners. Later Mercy and Dolly moved back to Alton Barnes to teach themselves in the school where their father had been master for so many years. I visited them when I was about twelve while staying with a school friend who lived in a neighbouring village. I remember walking back to Woodborough after tea with them on a black November afternoon. It brought to mind a rather interesting little story I heard my father tell. Once while in his teens he was cycling along this very road in the dark when he was suddenly surrounded by a myriad of tiny green lights – the eyes of rats, migrating from one farm to another, in an enormous horde. He pedalled on, rats to the right and rats to the left and was quite shaken by the experience. I was to tell this tale to many classes when we would discuss rats and grounds for truth in the legend of the Pied Piper. This same road was said to be haunted by the ghost of a headless lady, which appeared on moonlight nights. Father claimed to have seen the ghost many times, but overcame his fear to decide that the moon shining through two trees caused the apparition.

Only a few years ago, long after Mercy and Dolly had retired and died, I spent a day in the tiny school of Alton Barnes, at the invitation of a friend who was teaching there. I talked to the twenty odd pupils there of life in America, in the very same room where my father had sat, an eager pupil, some seventy years previously. Both Mildenhall and Alton Barnes schools are closed now in an effort through regionalization to make education more efficient and money go further. But there is no doubt in my mind, that those tiny village schools served isolated communities well and in the hands of dedicated teachers were fine institutions of primary learning.

Chapter VI

My mother and father were, I believe, largely unaware of how much they helped us get ready for school and provided for us culturally throughout childhood. They seemed to do the right things by instinct. They were also driven by the urge to give us a better start in life and more opportunity than they had had themselves – upward mobility on a small scale.

Though my mother left school at fourteen and my father even earlier, they both spoke clearly and correctly, had excellent vocabularies and could read and write with fluency and accuracy. I kept the letters that my mother wrote me after my arrival in New York in February 1946. She only lived two and a half months after my departure from home so they are few. Re-reading them, as I have many times, I am impressed by their clarity and lucidity. More importantly they are models in the art of intimate communication. Her handwriting was pretty and distinctive and there is no spelling or grammatical error of any kind. My father's style was more florid but his rare letters would contain Biblical, classical and literary allusions.

At home, we kept up with the events of the day through newspapers, periodicals and by radio. The politically conservative and imperialistic *Daily Express*, one of Lord Beaverbrook's publications, was delivered to the house in time for breakfast perusal by Father. He liked us to look at the newspaper but he was adamant that it was to be returned to him in good order. On this point, he was very touchy. When very young, we were mostly concerned with the daily adventures of 'Rupert', the little bear whose exploits written in simple verse brought joy to thousands of British children. The *Sunday Express* was an expanded version of its daily counterpart and was mildly sensational though nothing like *The People* or *The News of the World*. Mother enjoyed the Sunday paper – she read it while we were out walking with Father. Dad subscribed to *The Woodworker* and *The Connoisseur*, the latter a beautifully illustrated magazine about antiques. This was a rare extravagance and he enjoyed it very much, hoarding his copies till the day he died and becoming increasingly knowledgeable about all aspects of dealing in antiques. Mother, to our regret, did not take a woman's magazine. We would steal covert glances at *Home Chat* and *Woman's Own* at friends' houses and on our visits to the barber. The latter were rare, however, for in the interests of economy Mother usually cut our hair.

In the early 1920s, Dad was an enthusiastic experimenter with radio or the 'wireless' as it is known in England. He first built a crystal set, working up by degrees to something he called a super-heterodyne. We did not like the wireless at first for when he was attempting to listen in and bring in various stations, absolute silence was the rule and we were sharply reprimanded and sometimes slapped if we did not concur. Mother liked it no better for building wireless sets meant wiring and confusion, soldering and frustration and goodbye to peaceful evenings around the fire. I remember once telling Dad I could hear a station through the earphones when I could not, because I sensed how great his disappointment would be, but I also recall the thrill I got from hearing 'Radio Luxembourg' for the first time. We had an aunt who lived near Daventry, the first and largest radio transmitting station in England, and I was duly impressed by the forest of radio masts though I remained ignorant of their workings in spite of Dad's best efforts to enlighten me.

Later when radio got over its growing pains and we had acquired a loudspeaker, we listened to it regularly. We enjoyed the Childrens' Hour from 5 to 6p.m. for many years. This programme presented good children's literature, plays, music, songs and informational trivia and exposed us to the fine diction which has always been the hallmark of the B.B.C. The announcers on this programme were designated 'uncles'. One popular feature was the announcement of birthdays. Imagine my surprise when staying with an aunt in the Midlands when I heard my name announced with instructions to look for a gift in Sheila's basket. Sheila was my aunt's chocolate brown toy Pomeranian and sure enough, there I found a small china doll prettily dressed in white and purple gingham. Some fifteen years later, the headmaster at the first school I taught at in Birmingham, had been 'Uncle Bill' on the Midland Station in those early days of radio and I always cherished the illusion that it was he who had directed me to Sheila's basket.

As we grew older, Mother required us to listen to certain programmes which she judged informational and inspirational. When operas were presented, she would send to the B.B.C. for the librettos and we would follow the stories carefully. I believe Mother had gained her knowledge of and interest in opera from Mrs. Hume, her employer before her marriage. She also knew quite a lot about classical music and in contemporary music she had two great favourites, Ralph Vaughan Williams and Frederick Delius. This latter she admired greatly and told us many times how he continued to compose in spite of blindness and excruciating pain. Just recently I saw on television a movie about Delius that claimed his blindness was caused by the syphilis which eventually killed him. My first horrified reaction was one of gladness, that my mother never knew her idol had feet of clay.

Chapter VII

Crouched where the open upland billows down
Into the valley where the river flows,
She is as any other country town
That little lives or marks or hears or knows,

So, of Marlborough, wrote Charles Hamilton Sorley, an old Marlburian who lost his life in the Great War. In this poem entitled 'Marlborough' he goes on to describe the awareness of life and the dawn of knowledge that came to him in the streets, fields and forests of this little Wiltshire town.

Marlborough lies in a hollow in the downs on the banks of the Kennet, a tributary of the Thames. Except in the west, in order to get in or out of the town a hill has to be descended or ascended. The London road to the east and the Salisbury road to the south both pass through Savernake Forest, while the Pewsey road to the southwest rises up Granham Hill to the edge of the downs and then sharply descends Oare Hill into the fertile farmland of the Pewsey Vale. The Swindon road rises steeply to the Common, north of the town and then takes off straight as a die – the Romans had laid the first road – across the high exposed plateau of the Marlborough Downs. Only to the west is the road out of the town flat and straight – its straightness once again a legacy of the Romans – leading ultimately to Bath and Bristol. Leaving Marlborough it passes Preshute Church, through the low-lying watermeadows of the River Kennet until it reaches Beckhampton of racing stable fame. Here the road forks and rises gently to the high downland area leading to Devizes, if one takes the south fork and to Calne and Chippenham, if one takes the north branch.

To the north of the town lay the Common, land which belonged to all the townspeople, being a relic of the open field and land apportionment system of the Middle Ages. Theoretically, any townsman could use the land in his own way, as long as he did not infringe on the rights of others. We would see the odd cow grazing there and an occasional horse, donkey or goat tethered on this common land. When, in my childhood, a golf course was constructed on the Common, it was only after prolonged discussion as to whether it would use a large portion of common land for the privileged few. The course was eventually laid out but its facilities were available for any residents who wished to use them and pedestrians still had the right to walk across the course whether a game was in progress or not.

During World War II, the rights of the common man bowing to the national emergency, an army hospital was constructed there, the quonset huts of which were used for several years afterwards by the Secondary Modern School.

Prior to the making of the golf course, the Common was an open stretch of level heath covered in thick tough grass with occasional clumps of purple heather and thorny yellow gorse. It was the home of rabbits and hares and birds, like the curlew, flew overhead uttering their mournful, desolate cries. There in the spring the delicate lavender blue harebells waved in the breeze that always seemed to be blowing and at the far end of the Common some two miles away, was 'The Clump' – a small grove of larch trees crowning a slight eminence.

Sometimes our Sunday afternoon rambles with Father would take us across the Common to 'The Clump', a long walk from which we would return tired and with cheeks reddened by the cold winds to find Sunday tea in front of a roaring fire more than usually welcome.

Living in Marlborough from infancy, I cannot remember a time when I did not think it a very special place in which to live. My father first painted its ancient story for me in glowing colours and as I went to school much of our history, geography and nature learning sprang from the small town and its environs. Its story, assembled piece by piece in my mind like a jigsaw puzzle, gradually took shape and gave me my first awareness of time and history. In common with many of the town's residents, we took great pride in the fact that Marlborough was most ancient in an ancient land, that her first settlement was the huts of the area inhabited by early man and that she was rightly dubbed the gateway to Ancient Britain.

We early speculated on the various theories as to the meaning of the name. Was it Merlin's borough, in accordance with the legend that the Arthurian wise man Merlin was buried beneath Marlborough's mound? The town bears as its motto 'Ubi nunc sapientis ossa Merlini' – 'Where now are the bones of the wise Merlin.' Or did 'marl' refer to the chalk subsoil of Marlborough and its downs? Probably the most likely explanation is that it referred to the mound in the College grounds. Maerl was possibly an ancient British chief who erected the mound as a burial place for himself. Five miles to the west of Marlborough stands Silbury Hill, the largest man-made mound in the world. Since the Roman road, generally straight as an arrow, bends around it, the mound obviously pre-dates the Romans. Marlborough's mound is similar to Silbury, of approximately the same date, though considerably smaller. But Marlborough's mound was off limits for us for it stands within the confines of Marlborough College. We could only glimpse its tree-clad mystery from the top of Granham Hill, though once when a summer fete was held in the college grounds, my father and I climbed the winding path to the top where the Norman kings had built a castle now long since destroyed.

On the high chalk uplands of the Marlborough Downs are found many ancient British barrows or burial mounds, though none so large as those of Sil and Maerl. The excavation of these barrows has yielded rich treasures of the Stone and Bronze Ages – arrowheads, weapons, pottery and jewellery. Most of these are housed and documented in Devizes Museum to which we went several times as children. My most recent visit there was in 1977 along with my husband and a Marlborough friend.

Five miles away and adjacent to Silbury Hill was the Great British Temple of Avebury, both larger and older, though not as well known as Stonehenge. One great antiquarian, John Aubrey, said comparing Stonehenge to Avebury was like comparing a parish church to a cathedral. The temple, much decimated by the use of the stones as building material in the Middle Ages, consisted originally of great Sarsen monoliths set up in a series of concentric circles and avenues covering several miles of downland and thought to be a representation of a serpent, sacred symbol of many early peoples.

During my college years, I wrote a paper for my history studies on Avebury, its history and possible meaning. This happened in 1937 at a time when much excavation and restoration was going on under the direction of Alexander Keiller, scion of the great jam and marmalade company – and a brilliant archaeologist. I was privileged to share to a very limited extent in his work and I learned immensely from him. My paper was later borrowed by my history lecturer to read at a London historical society and was unfortunately lost. Today Avebury is one of the showplaces of Ancient Britain. Perhaps I should mention that the temple is not Avebury's only claim to fame. It was for a time the home of Dr. Edward Jenner, discoverer of vaccination as a prevention against smallpox and perhaps it was the beautiful unpocked complexions of West Country dairymaids that gave him the first clue in his research.

The Romans left fewer traces in Marlborough itself than did the earlier inhabitants, though there was a relatively important military settlement known as Cunetio to the northeast, near the village of Mildenhall (Minal). A carving of the Roman goddess Fortuna, much defaced, was found on a stone used in the building of St. Mary's Church, and I remember walking with my class from St. Mary's School to view it, along with later historical features. The straight road leading westward out of Marlborough towards Bath, followed the original Roman road and another stretch of Roman road lay between Marlborough and Swindon to the north.

After the last of the Roman legions was recalled to Rome in A.D. 407, Marlborough, along with many other places in the country, entered a period about which little is known. There is some evidence that a rudimentary Saxon settlement grew up around the grassy plots known as the Green hard by St. Mary's Church. We had to walk through the Green on our way to St. Mary's School. The Green was then, as now, graced by lovely Georgian houses, a far cry from the rude huts of the earliest English.

The first written evidence of Marlborough occurs in 1087, when the Domesday Book, a property record of his conquest, was mandated by the first Norman king, William the Conqueror. It is known that Marlborough, part of Wessex and as such loyal to Saxon Harold, came under the Conqueror's authority as early as 1067, only a year after the Battle of Hastings. A castle, a wooden structure which was superseded by a stone one, was erected on Marlborough's mound. The castle belonged to the king and much of the area of the town and its immediate environs became Crown property. There was a royal mint at Marlborough during Norman days and Marlborough pennies from those times are rare museum pieces today. The Norman kings and their successors hunted in Savernake Forest before the famous New Forest in Hampshire was developed into a royal hunting preserve.

Marlborough Castle was a favourite residence of King John of Magna Carta fame or rather infamy. He was married in Marlborough to Isabella of Gloucester (1190) and it is said that some of his children were born in the castle and christened in the rare and beautiful font of black stone that stands today in Preshute Church. The font probably stood then in the castle chapel of St. Nicholas but was later moved to Preshute which was built as a garrison church for the soldiers and villeins of the castle. Preshute is a church without a village and the name is thought to be a corruption of 'Pres Chateau' – 'Near the Castle.'

Henry III, King John's oldest son and successor, held his last parliament in Marlborough in 1267 and a noteworthy law, known as the Statute of Marlborough, was passed there. As Magna Carta gave rights and privileges to the barons, so the Statute of Marlborough categorically stated the rights of small landowners. Legend has it that this law was passed in a building standing on the site of the present day Merlin restaurant. It was in this restaurant that our wedding reception was held on 15 March 1944.

In 1204 King John granted Marlborough a charter making it a royal borough. The Normans built a church where the present St. Mary's stands, though the only evidence of their church is a solid oak door heavily studded and set in a series of the round arches beloved by the Normans and decorated with their favourite dog-tooth design. Preshute too was built at this time, though of the original building, only parts of the tower survive.

For the next three hundred years, the little town grew and prospered, though slowly as medieval towns did. Henry VIII's marriage to Jane Seymour, who lived at Wolfhall nearby and the subsequent birth of her son Edward VI, though it cost her her life, re-established Marlborough firmly in royal favour. In 1550, the Grammar School was founded by Edward VI.

In the seventeenth century during the Civil War (1642–1651), Marlborough by virtue of its geographical position was a bone of contention between the Royalists and the Roundheads. The town sympathies, surprisingly so in view of Marlborough's royal connections, were almost wholly with the Parliamentarians. This was due largely to resentment against the levying of Ship Money, a heavy tax for building ships for the Navy. However the landed nobility of the surrounding area were strong supporters of the king. The town was stormed and taken by the Royalists on 5 December 1642. The defenders stubbornly resisted in St. Mary's Church but were eventually taken prisoner. Subsequently the town changed hands several times with grievous damage. Marks of pistol, musket ball and cannon shot can still be seen in the church towers.

With the Civil War barely over, there occurred in 1653 the first of a series of devastating fires. The town was well nigh destroyed – churches, houses, public buildings almost a total loss. It was the last fire that gave Marlborough its most distinctive and charming characteristic – its wide High Street – many say the widest in all England. Prior to the fire there had been two narrow streets running parallel with houses back to back between the two, where now car park and the bi-weekly market is held. After the last fire, the houses in the centre were not rebuilt. Today the Town Hall stands in the centre of the High Street at its east end, while at the west end stands St. Peter's Church with its coffin-shaped churchyard flanked on either side by the divided High Street.

The fire that destroyed St. Mary's Church gave rise to one little tale much beloved by Marlborough residents. A cat is said to have gone back into the burning belfry repeatedly to bring out her kittens alive, losing her own life in the process. When the church was rebuilt a carving of the heroic feline was tucked up under the eaves where gargoyles are usually to be found. Generations of Marlborough school children, myself among them, have walked the linden avenue leading through the Green to the church to attempt to distinguish the form of the cat among several much eroded animal figures and then returned to school to write up for their English composition exercise an account of the cat who gave up her life for her kittens.

Edward VI who ruled from 1546–1553 was the last royal owner of Marlborough Castle. The royal properties passed on his death into the hands of his mother's family, the Seymours. The castle itself, gradually fell into ruin but in the latter half of the seventeenth century, a Seymour built a new mansion nearby. This in turn was replaced by the present building which first served as a Seymour residence, later became the Castle Inn and is today 'C' House of Marlborough College. Its Georgian façade viewed from the Bath road, through iron gates and a long avenue of trees is a joy to behold. As the Castle Inn, it enjoyed a period of great prosperity in the coaching days, when it had the reputation of being the finest hostelry between London and Bath. William Pitt (1708–1778), Pitt the Elder, Earl of Chatham and Prime Minister of England spent two weeks there, crippled by the gout and Stanley Weyman wrote his most famous novel entitled *The Castle Inn* about it.

But the coming of the railways ended the days of the stage coach and the Inn's prosperity rapidly decreased. In 1838 it was bought by the Reverend Charles Plater to found a school for the sons of clergymen. Thus Marlborough College gained its start and 'C' House has remained the nucleus and focal point of one of the most prestigious of England's public schools.

Today Marlborough is a rather sleepy little town basking in the fame of its past history. Quite a prosperous entity in herself, she has always counted heavily on her position on the main London–Bath-Bristol road. Being seventy-five miles west of London makes her a good stopping place for through traffic, and the wide High Street offers ample space for free parking with easy access to her shops among which there is a preponderance of cafes and restaurants to feed the weary traveller. Such popularity has inevitably brought its own traffic problems and on summer weekends motorists often face the twin bottlenecks of ingress and egress. When the M4 motorway between London and South Wales bypassed Marlborough, going instead from Hungerford to Swindon, there were dire fears of what it would do to Marlborough's carriage trade. To the best of my knowledge Marlborough is surviving nicely. Her fame as a fine stopping place, her beauty and history, lure the discriminating traveller to take the old road, or make the short detour from the motorway, and many pleasure tours retain Marlborough on their itineraries for the reasons mentioned above. Under the circumstances she now appears to have enough rather than too much traffic.

Between the two wars, Marlborough grew considerably and several housing estates, low cost but not unattractive, were built on her perimeters. During World War II her facilities were strained and swollen by evacuees and military personnel, but at the same time she enjoyed a spurious war time prosperity, again largely by virtue of her geographical position. After the war, a housing shortage persisted, and the town fathers saw fit to open up the alleys and lanes running from the lower side of the High Street down to the River Kennet. Close and dark with tiny houses crowded together, these alleys had bordered on slums but now with dwellings expanded, combined and renovated, and roadways widened, they form attractive adjuncts to the town.

The Priory, one of the many fine High Street houses, was left by its owner to the town, and the extensive gardens leading down to the river have now become a public park, with wide lawns, fine herbaceous borders and spreading trees, making it a source of enjoyment to visitor and resident alike. Part of St. Mary's churchyard has also been converted into a park, the chipped and broken gravestones restored and laid flush in the thick green turf, a quiet place where people can experience a few moments of contemplation and reflection as they turn for a brief space from the cares of the world. At the opposite end of the High Street, St. Peter's Church, its pulpit once the scene of the thundering sermons of Dr. Sacheverell, is no longer used for services but has become a meeting place for youth and church groups, musical and dramatic societies, and is in addition a centre for brass rubbing, a hobby much in vogue in England today.

Marlborough's schools have also changed. The anitquated buildings of the church schools are abandoned for educational purposes, though St. Peter's school now houses the Public Library. Junior children today receive their instruction in the building that, in my day, was Marlborough Grammar School, while the Grammar School, bowing to progress and now comprehensive, divides its student body by age between the newer buildings on Granham Hill and off the Mildenhall Road. Marlborough College has grown closer to the town – there is greater communication, more sharing of ideas, and facilities with the town schools. Scholarships are offered to native youth, the school has gone co-educational and the dress code is relaxed. Truly the old order changeth.

When I return to Marlborough now I walk along its High Street and, sadly, see hardly a soul I know. Though many of the shops, which I once thought permanent landmarks, have changed hands and character, I do not feel a stranger. The wide street, a church at either end, and the Town Hall abutting into it, remains the same, dear to my heart for the memories evoked and I feel I have come home.

Chapter VIII

Marlborough's history, of course, was England's in microcosm and much of both local and national history I absorbed as by osmosis and gradually with the help of my father and my teachers began to see it in chronological and geographical perspective.

History was all around us. We played among the ruins of St. Margaret's monastery, a stone's throw from where we lived. We used to cross the road to chat with the blacksmith whose smithy stood on the corner of Salisbury Road and George Lane. His name was Stephen Looker though we always properly addressed him as Mr. Looker – and all the neighbourhood children loved him and his wife. They were childless – a great sorrow to him as the smithy had been handed down from father to son for many generations. He liked to tell how one of his ancestors had refused to shoe Oliver Cromwell's horse – unlike most of the townsfolk, he must have been a King's man. Oliver Cromwell had stayed in the George Inn opposite the smithy. In my childhood, it was a decrepit, though once beautiful, Tudor building but has since been pulled down and replaced by the Roman Catholic Church of St. Thomas More.

When small girls, we would often walk the lane known as 'round the mill' to get to Father's garage and workshop. We would have to cross the wooden lady bridge, soon replaced by a metal one, past the medieval mill building and the lovely old house and outbuildings that housed Morrison's rope factory – a small industry that had been in existence for over two hundred years. We were free to roam, walk and picnic among the great beeches and oaks of Savernake Forest, where William the Conqueror hunted and Henry VIII courted Jane

Seymour. The forest was part of the ancestral estate of the Marquess of Ailesbury and he offered its use freely to the public. We often wandered through the watermeadows of the Kennet to Preshute Church. We liked to read the epitaphs on the tombstones and like Thomas Gray wonder about the lives of those cut short by death. Now my mother, father and sister all lie buried in that peaceful spot. All the churches were open for us to enter for a quiet moment of reflection. It was good to grow up in a place where we could walk with history.

It was good too, to grow up in a college town. The gulf was great when we were young, but even so we glimpsed the life and education of the wealthy and privileged. We used to see the boys around town in their striped trousers, black coats and Eton caps, the prefects being the only ones permitted to carry umbrellas. We would listen with something like awe to their upper class, well-bred voices. In the fields and forest, we would see them practising for their cross country races in shorts and singlets and every so often the O.T.C. would march past with flags flying and band playing. Prize Day in July was always a big day in Marlborough. The town was full of well-dressed parents and sisters of the boys, the High Street lined with lovely cars and Marlborough's resources were strained to the utmost to house and feed the visitors. Marlborough merchants counted heavily on Prize Day. For several years as I was growing up, I sold Queen Alexandra Roses for charity, in the High Street on Prize Day Saturday. One year dressed in pink with a big white hat with velvet ribbon, I remember drawing many admiring glances and taking in an unusually large amount of money.

Marlborough is a beautiful town with a melange of architectural styles melded into a harmonious whole. I wish I could write that I lived in one of the Marlborough's many beautiful homes, but such was not the case. We lived in one of a row of ten tall narrow houses facing the main London–Bath road where it is intersected with the Salisbury Road. The houses backed up onto the River Kennet. The river was crystal clear in those days, speckled trout, ducks and moorhens could often be seen, and at the bottom of our strip of garden, there was a willow fringed island that was the subject of some romantic fantasies when I was young. When in school as a five-year-old, I learned to parrot Rose Fyleman's trite little verse 'There are fairies at the bottom of our garden,' I felt sure she was referring to our island. Unfortunately, on the opposite bank of the river, stood the town gas works which rather marred the idyllic scene and occasionally polluted the pure bracing air for which Marlborough was noted.

The houses in the row, known as Bridge Buildings, had been built around 1900. They were small and cramped and since they were built around a curve, some of the rooms were oddly shaped. Our front door entered a narrow dark hall with the sitting room to the left and the small living room straight ahead. Beyond that there was a brick floored kitchen or scullery, as we called it, and then came the copper, where the washing was done and then a lavatory. There was no bathroom – I think my mother felt fortunate to have inside toilet facilities. There were four bedrooms, two on the second floor and two on the third. The sitting room and my parents' bedroom were the most pleasant rooms in the house. The sitting room, which after I had left home, was made into my father's shop, was only used on Sundays and holidays. My mother's bedroom was light and sunny, and she spent a lot of time sewing and reading there in the warmer weather. Only in cases of rather severe illness, was a fire lighted in the bedroom and then the patient was moved in to Mother's bed and other sleeping arrangements were made for everyone else. I liked to sit at the window of her room, like the Lady of Shallot, and watch the world go by, but I needed no mirror and it was many years before Sir Lancelot appeared.

The room in which we did most of our living was rather small and dark. It was heated by an open fireplace which replaced a black stove. I can dimly remember my mother getting up early to 'blacklead' this stove and how happy she was when this unpleasant chore was eliminated. My sister and I shared the bedroom over this room and the two rooms at the top, were used for storage. The larger of the two was our playroom and was used sometimes as an extra bedroom.

Mother cooked by gas for which she paid by putting shillings in the meter in the hall. At first the house was lighted by gas, but electricity was brought in when I was about seven. Mother did not like being billed for what we had used every quarter. I think she was afraid of running up a bill too big to pay. Consequently she was most strict about putting out lights and made us continue to use candles at bedtime. I did much of my reading by candlelight after I went to bed, so it was no wonder that I was wearing glasses by the time I was eleven.

Looking back from the vantage point of the lovely labour-saving houses I have lived in in America, I shudder to think of the inconveniences, draughts, steps in odd places, dark curving stairs, no hot water or bathroom, no heat, that my mother had to endure. Yet our house was always sparkling clean and the most marvellous meals and dishes came out of the little black stove.

Comparatively, too, we had some interesting and valuable possessions, though I am afraid I realised this too late, so that I have only a few left me today. In the hall, we had two enormous lithographs – one was of Aurora driving her chariot across heaven and the other showed Laocoon in his death throes. Hanging over the door to the living room was a pair of horns from a Highland steer mounted complete with shaggy black hair. A narrow oak table and a tiny oak chair with a heart motif, both made by my father, were all the furniture there was room for. The sitting room was the showplace for my father's fine masterpieces and in addition there was a three-piece suite of upholstered furniture. The floor was covered with a patterned Wilton carpet in muted colours. There were several beautiful porcelain vases on display and some silver pieces of sentimental value that Mother prized. She also had a rather impressive collection of Gosse china. This was made up of small useless pieces decorated with coats of arms of different towns and cities, and bought as souvenirs of holiday visits by oneself or received as gifts from friends. I did not like this collection, regarding it as evidence of bourgeois taste. In other ways, I thought my mother's taste impeccable. Today, the Gosse collection would be quite valuable, but that too escaped me, and it really is one thing whose disappearance I do not regret.

We had a large Welsh dresser which was one of the few things my father had inherited from his family, along with a beautiful little Sheraton washstand – a collector's item – and a lovely round polished table in Mother's bedroom. We had some fine pictures too. In the living room, there was a large coloured print of Sir John Millais' picture 'When did you last see your Father?' in which a Cavalier child is being interrogated by Cromwell's soldiers and another picture was titled 'The Elopement' in which an English squire is trying to find his missing daughter. We had some good hunting prints and two Landseer pictures of dogs and red deer which had belonged to Grandfather Sharpe. We also had two lovely watercolours of the Austrian Tyrol matted in gold and beautifully framed. Another watercolour, in my possession today, was very special to my mother. It was of the house in Great Cheverell where my mother had lived when the family left Herefordshire and where her father had died. It was painted by Miss Grant-meek, daughter of my father's employer at the time, and given to my parents as a wedding present.

When I was about eight, my parents made a very special purchase that had taken them years to save enough money to buy. It was a piano – a fine upright of glossy mahogany with ivory keys. It was sent down from London and the day of its arrival was a red-letter one indeed.

Both my sister and I began to take lessons. Miss Collins, who had taught us in the Infants' School was our teacher and every Saturday morning we would walk the length of the High Street for half-an-hour of instruction in her little dark house in the shadow of St. Peter's Church. Miss Collins was fortyish, a spinster who had once been pretty, a talented woman who had become an uncertificated teacher to support her parents, her father Irish and her mother a London Jewess. They had left London and moved to Marlborough at the beginning of the Great War. Miss Collins and my mother were good friends and she often visited us for tea on Sundays. She was a good piano teacher and for her efforts charged a shilling for thirty minutes. Our lessons were disrupted for a while by her illness. She had to go to London to undergo a mastectomy but returned to teach in good health for several years before succumbing to her disease.

We were to Mother's disappointment only average piano students. My sister had more musical talent than I, but would not practice, while my more conscientious work was not enough to make up for the lack of ability. But both of us learned to play after a fashion, and I found my knowledge of the instrument most useful in teaching both in England and America.

The piano, too, gave us many evenings of pleasure whenever a pianist was among the friends who visited us. Then the rafters rang with the singing of hymns, the good old folk songs of England, and the sentimental ditties of World War I, occasionally interspersed with some of the popular songs of the thirties.

Chapter IX

In common with other dwellings of modest size in the England of my childhood, the only form of heat was the open fireplace, in which coal was a fuel preferred over wood. In order to ensure a sufficient supply of coal, my mother had to budget carefully. If my memory serves me correctly, she, more providently than many of our neighbours, bought a hundredweight (112 pounds) of coal every other week summer as well as winter. Thus at the beginning of winter, we had a nice stock of fuel in, and this was carefully used and supplemented by waste wood from my father's workshop. The coal was stored in an area beyond the copper, inelegantly though aptly known as the coal hole. During most of my years at home, the coal was brought round in a horsedrawn cart, bagged up in hundredweight sacks and delivered into the coal hole by the coalman, Mr. Witt. He was a middle-aged man, his back bent by years of carrying coal sacks, his hands and his face begrimed with coal dust from which peered a pair of startling blue eyes. When we saw him on Sundays clean and dressed in his best for church, it came as a shock to realize what a handsome face it was. Mother always liked a little chat with him, and provided a cup of tea for him, and he would ask after us if we were at school and exchange pleasantries wih us if we were at home. He was, I suppose, one of Nature's gentlemen, who for lack of opportunity, was locked into a menial, unpleasant and backbreaking job, perhaps counting himself fortunate to have a job of any kind in the depressed twenties. His work-weary horse would stand patiently waiting for him to complete his deliveries before plodding on once more on the rounds. The horse went, I think, without any direction from him, always stopping at the right places.

The coal, most of which came from South Wales, varied in quality as well as in price though there was not necessarily a relationship between the two. Sometimes Mother would declare the coal was mostly shale and dust and then the fire burned smokily and half-heartedly. At other times it was shiny black anthracite which burned brightly and gave out a lovely heat, though that made Mother complain that it was burning too fast and she would never be able to make it last. We were never, however caught without fuel as some people were. The fact that we always started the winter with a full coal hole made us proof against strikes and delivery problems due to weather vagaries.

Among the older people, there was a tradition, probably born of the necessity for economy, never to light a fire before 1 November or after 1 April, regardless of the weather. Mother tried to keep this in mind but in times of bitter cold we always had a fire. Many women in the town had a little hand-drawn cart which they would take into Savernake Forest on 'wooding' expeditions. For some reason while doing this chore, they would always wear a discarded cap belonging to their husbands – the typical tweed cap beloved by the British working man. The women always wore it back to front. We were glad that Mother never had to resort to such measures. Wood for us was fairly plentiful though, compared with coal, it is an inefficient source of heat and so we only used it as a supplement.

Mother would get up first to light the fire on coal-dark winter mornings. She would start it by rolling sheets of newspaper into tubes and tying them into bows. Once the fire had started and the kettle was boiling, then the rest of the family would appear for breakfast. If she had trouble starting the fire she would often blame the weather saying the wind was in the wrong direction. I do not know if there was any truth in this assertion.

Though we had three fireplaces in the house, normally only one fire was lighted. Sunday afternoons when we had visitors and on Christmas Day, the sitting room fire was lighted and in cases of severe illness one was put in Mother's bedroom. During the summer months the fireplaces were hidden by ornamental wood screens carved or inlaid by my father. Such screens were big sellers and there were many in the town which were made by him.

Another annual visitation determined by our use of open fires was that of the chimney sweep. In the late spring Mother would send a note to Mr. Bull, the sweep, to arrange a date with him. It was an event as much dreaded by all of us, though most of all by my mother, as that of honey extraction. The day before the sweep came everything that could be, was moved out of the living room and everything that could not be, was covered with dust sheets. The sweep's work was normally done in the very early hours of the morning and he always came to our house between 4 and 5a.m. Newspapers were laid out to catch the stray soot and he set vigorously to work with his circular brushes. They varied in size, the smallest going to the top of the chimney and the handles of the brushes screwing one into the other. We used to lie in bed and listen to the thundering noise the brushes made as he rotated them to clear out the black soot lining the flues, some of it caked on and very hard to dislodge. His bags caught most of it and the newspapers some of the rest but it was a dirty job and after he had left walls, windows and floor were swept, washed and polished. The furniture, pictures and bric-a-brac were all cleaned before being returned to their places and curtains and covers were laundered and ironed. The visit of the sweep coincided with spring cleaning and we were always glad when it was over and things, including Mother's temper, returned to normal. Mother was always punctilious about having the sweep for she was deathly afraid that the chimney would catch on fire – a frightening experience and one that could precipitate a fire of alarming proportions. Living in a row of houses as we did, one of Mother's worries was over neighbours who had a less responsible attitude to chimney sweeping.

The sweep, Mr. Bull, the only one in the town and so indispensable, was quite a well-known character. He was a short squat strongly built man, said to be of gypsy extraction, whom we would see striding from house to house with his brushes on his back and his face black as the ace of spades from the soot. He always had a cheery word, smile and wave for us but as small children we were rather scared of him. I think I always suspected him of sending small boys up the chimney as was once done in England. We had read Charles Kingsley's *The Water Babies* at school and the agonies of Little Tom, the chimney boy, made a profound impression on me.

Once the chimney had been swept Mother was quite reluctant to have another fire and only in cases of extremely unseasonable weather was one lighted. Then she felt we could start the cold weather with a clean chimney and go through the winter without the possibility of a chimney fire.

Chapter X

Marlborough lies in the heart of England's racing country. There are many stables nearby breeding and training horses for the sport of kings. Fifty odd years ago, when I was a child, we would often see long strings of horses being ridden or led to the railway station en route to racemeets at Salisbury, Newbury or Ascot. The skittish creatures could be unnerved by a lorry or loud car. The stable lads – 'lads' cared for the horses and rode them to exercise as opposed to 'jockeys' who rode them in the races – were often hard put to control them. Sometimes a horse would rear up and canter wildly, its hooves striking sparks from the sidewalk. Such excitability, being highly infectious, often a whole string of horses would become nervous and volatile. I was always very frightened of the horses and was glad when their trips to the railway station grew less and less as more and more stables purchased the huge ungainly vehicles known as horseboxes and transported their animals by road.

On Saturday nights, Marlborough and its pubs were always crowded with very small but very tough young men – the 'lads' from the nearby stables out on the town. Small stature was a prerequisite for the job and many lads dieted strenuously to keep their weight down. A lot of the lads were Irish, speaking with an accent so strong that they could barely be understood, while others came from the poor areas of the large cities up north. Few were local boys. It was the dream of every 'lad' to become a 'jockey'. Not many did and because youth was the name of the game, most eventually found other employment though some became 'head' lads, positions with considerable responsibility in the stables. One 'lad' who attained fame, fortune, and a knighthood into the bargain, was Sir Gordon Richards, who made his home in Marlborough for many years.

Ex-stable lads often drifted into the peripheral activities of racing – betting and tipping. The pubs of Marlborough were always full of racing people and many were the 'tips' vouchsafed over the 'pints'. Racing fever reached its height in Derby and Ascot weeks. Our next door neighbours were racing people and very occasionally Mother would get a hot tip and bet a shilling each way on a horse. Even more occasionally the horse would win and then we enjoyed the extra pennies which appeared to us to have literally fallen from heaven.

It was the chalkdowns around Marlborough that gave rise to the horseracing industry. The short springy turf covering the low rounded hills made excellent gallops and training grounds for the horses. Another connected industry was that of leather and saddle making. Marlborough still is the home of a tannery and small rope industry and a family named Chandler have had a saddlery business in the town for generations.

Today I read and enjoy the mystery stories of Dick Francis set as they are in the world of horse racing.

Chapter XI

Autumn brought two fairs to Marlborough, held from time immemorial and, for reasons unknown, on the Saturdays before and after October 11. Marlborough's fairs are unusual because they are held in the very wide High Street, the use of which, for two twenty-four hour periods annually, had been granted to the fair people by special charter.

The fair people would begin drifting into the neighbourhood in their colourful caravans the week before coming from their previous stop, which I believe was Devizes. They were descendants of gypsies or Romanies, nomadic people with swarthy skins, oily black hair and a penchant for gold jewellery and gaudy colours. They were not welcome in the area, as they had the reputation for petty thievery and poaching. We were always warned never to speak to any of them or wander anywhere near the Common where their caravans, mostly at that time horsedrawn, were stationed. Actually the fair people were hardworking, diligent people conforming to a demanding schedule and reputation-wise, I think they were confused with wandering gypsies who had no steady means of livelihood, beyond selling clothes pins, repairing pots and pans and telling fortunes. Two or three caravans belonging to the latter people might arrive in the neighbourhood at any time and stay a few weeks, and they would send their children to the local school until they moved off again. These were the poachers, the petty thieves and larcenists who were most unwelcome. One old gypsy lady came to our house two or three times a year for many years, selling Mother clothes pins and telling fortunes from hands and the tealeaves left from the cup of tea Mother always provided for her. But Mother always strictly enjoined us to have nothing to do with gypsies and never to wander near their encampments.

Among the fair people, were some very wealthy families such as the Jennings of Devizes. This family, a veritable dynasty, appeared to have cornered the market of merry-go-rounds, roundabouts and pleasure rides. As small children, we were very partial to the great switchback whales in whose gigantic brightly coloured bellies, we would relax in red velvet comfort while we revolved at a not too startling speed. Some of the rides were labelled dangerous by my parents, so we never experienced the thrills of the roller coaster or the chair-o-planes. Several years ago, a bizarre accident occurred in which one of the chairs from this ride became detached and flew through a window of the Ailesbury Arms Hotel, killing the rider, but fortunately landing in an unoccupied room. Another real hazard during fair days was fire and this also occurred fairly recently in the High Street, with the fire engines unable to reach the conflagration because of the fair apparatus blocking the way. Small wonder that there is a movement on by the townspeople, merchants especially, to transfer the fair to the Common. It has so far been unsuccessful for tradition dies hard and the right to hold the fair in the High Street was granted centuries ago in a written charter. There is no doubt in my mind that the charm of Marlborough's fair lies in its High Street location and that on the Common it would cease to be in a matter of a few years.

In addition to the rides there were side shows, coconut shies, food stalls selling winkles (which Mother vetoed) and brandy snaps or fairings as they were called, which were permitted. Brown, sticky and rolled into lacy cylinders they melted in the mouth. There were also games of chance and competitions of many kinds. The chances of winning were rather remote but I did once acquire a goldfish which lived eleven years, and one year Father knocked so many coconuts down that he was asked to desist. Going back recently and staying in a hotel in the High Street during fair time, I felt that the fair had lost its glamour, appearing in all its tawdry raucousness but it was a magic time as a child. The familiar High Street was absolutely transformed with lights and music and crowds and walking along the lower side of the street where some of the caravans were drawn up one could catch tantalizing glimpses of gypsy domesticity. We used to save our pennies for weeks before the fair and added our prayers for fine weather to those of the fair people. Wet weather vastly increased their work and vastly decreased their profits.

The second and larger of the two fairs was known as 'Mop' fair and had originally been a hiring fair. Any farm labourer desirous of changing his place of employment would wear his appropriate symbol in his hat – i.e. a whip for a carter, straw for a thatcher, wool for a shepherd, etc. – and go to the fair where he was likely to be approached by a farmer on the lookout for a man of his particular skill. This custom was a relic of very long ago and did not entirely die out until after the First World War.

The fairs still continue in the High Street and those two Saturdays in October still bring the brassy raucous fair to the normally staid High Street. In spite of the inconvenience for the merchants and High Street dwellers I, for one, feel it a link with the past which must not be broken.

Chapter XII

Marlborough Sheep Fair was another fall diversion. For centuries the raising of sheep had been one of the most important elements of farming on the chalk downs, the short turf supporting the animals bred both for wool and meat. Until the industrial revolution the wool had been spun and woven in the local cottages but with the advent of machines the industry had moved to Yorkshire where coal, iron and good water were readily available. But sheep raising remained important to Wiltshire's downland farms.

Local farmers used to start bringing their flocks to the site of the fair, Marlborough Common, the day before and the sheep were kept there in pens until sale by auction. The pens were made of hurdles, sections of fence made by interlacing pliant strips of wood. A finished hurdle made by one of the old craftsmen was a thing of beauty and it is sad that today hurdle making is a rural art that has almost died out. As the sheep were sold, so they would be driven to their new homes. This meant that for the best part of three days, the roads in and out of the town and especially in the Common area were choked with huge flocks of sheep controlled by two or three drovers and a couple of sheep dogs usually of the collie breed. Sheep dog trials were sometimes held at the fair and prizes awarded to the best working dogs. As time went on more and more sheep were transported by lorry but when I was small they were driven in either by their farmer owners or by men whose profession was that of sheep driving. Known as drovers, they hired themselves out to take sheep from farm to farm, to market and to these regional fairs. The drovers were a breed all their own and we got to know some of them by sight as they appeared year after year at Sheep Fair. They always wore hob-nailed boots, leather gaiters, heavy brown work-coats, battered hats and carried heavy staves rather than the traditional shepherd's crook. Each drover had his dog and working together they made a perfect pair. Since they made good money at fairtime they visited the pubs in town in the evenings and much jollity and raucous singing ensued with an occasional altercation during which blows might be exchanged. They were a rowdy bunch.

One drover we always recognized – Old Bill. He was an old man who had been driving sheep all his long life. He always wore an old hat – a trilby without any indentation in the crown – it was his trademark – and he hobbled along leaning heavily on his staff. It was said of him that even in the 1920s he could drive a flock of sheep from Salisbury Plain to Stratford on Avon, almost a hundred miles, without going on a paved road.

Father, of course, was always at Sheep Fair with his employer who was one of the busiest auctioneers there, and Dad got to know some of the drovers whom he found very interesting. Not many people could understand their broad Wiltshire speech but Father could and could also reply in the same dialect. Once Dad took me to Sheep Fair and we stopped to talk to Old Bill. He said I was a right 'purty' little maid and gave me a sixpence – such generosity surprising Father greatly.

Sheep are very silly animals following their leader to the point of absurdity. I never liked to meet a flock. Once I saw a little boy knocked down by the lead sheep and every animal in the flock jumped over him. Fortunately he was unhurt, only very frightened. Sometimes one sheep would evade dogs and drover and all the rest would try to follow. The dogs would come flying around yapping and nipping until the sheep were back in flock formation. Some of the larger animals had a chemical on their fleece which turned it a bright orange. These were the rams, pedigree animals which would bring a high price, distinct from the ewes and lambs by their greater size as well as their coloured wool.

Chapter XIII

When I was five years old I went to London for the first time. The summer of 1923 was very hot and dry with drought conditions comparable with those of 1976 – quite rare in England. It was the year of the British Exhibition of Wembley. This huge fair, much like the later World Fairs and the Crystal Palace Exposition of Prince Albert in 1851, was organized with the hope that it would reinforce the ties of the Empire which had been somewhat strained by the war. It was also expected to inspire a national pride in the accomplishments of British people all over the world and hopefully would bring society back to something like pre-war normality.

We went on the train, travelling first on the branch line to Savernake, a hamlet on the main Great Western Railway line running from London to Bristol. The seventy-mile journey to London from Savernake took about two hours. We were all in our best, wearing hats, gloves, long-sleeved dresses in spite of the heat and my father in his Sunday navy blue serge suit and brown trilby hat and a high stiffly starched collar which was attached to his collarless shirt by a stud at the back of the neck. Unfortunately I discovered the hard way that I suffered from train sickness and just before we puffed into Paddington Station, I threw up. As my father bent over me his hat fell off and narrowly escaped disaster. However once on terra firma, I quickly recovered and taking a taxi to the Exhibition, made me feel very rich and important.

I cannot remember much of what I saw but a few things have stayed in my mind. There was an enormous statue of the boyish looking and very popular Prince of Wales sculpted in butter. I believe it was a contribution from New Zealand. Several years ago when in Penang, Malaysia, the Rasasayang Hotel where we were staying had on display a model of the Taj Mahal carved out of butter. It reminded me of my long ago visit to Wembley and I thought what a strange medium to sculpt in in a tropic country. Since Penang was for many years the resort and playground for

British Empire officials in the Far East, I also wondered if the craft of butter sculpture had any imperial significance.

We saw some large billed tropical birds known as toucans which came from British Guiana. These made an impression on me because my father, who had taken up marquetry as a hobby, had just completed a wood inlay of a toucan. In later years when teaching, I came to realize what a thrill children get when they learn something new in two different contexts. I also remember the pot of guava jelly my father bought at the Exhibition. Full of sugar crystals, I was less impressed with its taste than with the romance of its Oriental origin. When reading Kenneth Grahame's *The Wind in the Willows* to my classes, as I did many times, I always thought of our Wembley adventure when guava jelly was among the food rustled up by the badger after the rout of the weasels and the stoats.

We made a day trip to London almost every year during my childhood and were taken to see Westminster Abbey, the Houses of Parliament, Buckingham Palace, St. Paul's Cathedral, Madame Tussaud's and some of the museums and art galleries. Occasionally, we stayed for several days at a time with one of our uncles who lived in Hampstead. Father loved London and knew a great deal about it. Seeing it with him gave us a more penetrating view than most children of our day and class were able to get. As we grew older, we would go with Mother on shopping expeditions at sale time. It was always an occasion when we went 'to town'.

My two years of college in Putney on the south bank of the Thames gave me a further opportunity to enjoy London — its history, culture, sights and sounds. Wherever they may live, London occupies a very special place in the hearts of all English people.

Chapter XIV

In addition to living in a very ancient town and receiving an education heavily loaded with historical knowledge, there were other factors in our lives which reinforced and strengthened our sense of history.

We looked forward greatly to our annual trip to Tidworth Tattoo.

Tidworth, on Salisbury Plain and about fifteen miles from Marlborough, was one of the great army centres of the Southern
Command, and every August the regiments stationed there would
present the great military panoply known as a tattoo for the
entertainment of the general public. The tattoo was always held at
night so starting time was at 10.30 in the gathering dusk of the long
summer evenings. Tattoo night meant an attempt at an afternoon
nap and a light supper for we were always too excited to eat much.
We left early for the fifteen-mile drive for finding parking in the
grassy areas set aside for cars was time consuming. As always in
England before any outside activity, we prayed for fine weather
and our prayers must have been answered for I can remember no
occasion when the tattoo was washed out. The drive there was
great fun, largely because a late evening ride was so foreign to our
usual routine and I remember the thrill of finding our seats in the
growing darkness in the natural amphitheatre formed by the folds
of the chalk downs of the Plain where the tattoo was always
performed. I still get shivers up my spine when I hear British
military bands and see British soldiers marching, for no other men
have quite the precision, the finesse, the aplomb. The cavalry
regiments were always superb in their musical rides, their charging
gallops. Over the years we saw horses gradually superseded by
mechanization – the motorcycles, armoured cars and tanks and
those wonderful horses appeared less and less. They seemed so
much extensions of their riders that together they looked almost
one creature, updated versions of the centaurs of Greek mythology.
There was usually a Scottish regiment stationed at Tidworth and I
liked watching those ladies from Hell march, their kilts and spor-
rans swaying in time to the weird wailing of their bagpipes. One of
the highlights of every tattoo was the dramatisation of an epic
event in Britain's long military history. I remember seeing enact-
ments of the Battle of Hastings, the last cavalry charge at Omdur-
man, the Relief of Lucknow, the charge of the Light Brigade and
the Battle of Rorke's Drift. I was literally there, suffering, dying
and conquering with the flower of the British Empire. Call such
displays what you will – militaristic, anachronistic, out of touch
with the times – they gave me a rare kind of inspiration – pride in
England, her history, her past, her soldiers, her traditions and I
treasure the feeling of exaltation, the uplifting memories still.

Several times we attended British military shows in Madison
Square Garden in New York City and once we went to Edinburgh
Tattoo which is performed on the flloodlit Castle parade grounds.

The thrill still persists for me. In Edinburgh our younger son Chris was with us. It was in the rebellious sixties and he was eighteen, a freshman at Brown University. Something of a pacifist and a hater of the military he was, I know, thrilled with the show in spite of himself and I was glad for him to know and experience first hand, something that gave me so much delight when I was a child in England.

At one time during our childhood we used to visit a friend of my father, who for a brief time was stationed with his cavalry regiment at Tidworth. He was a sergeant and I have no idea how my father knew him or where he came from. He had a wife and two daughters and we exchanged visits. His name was Wilson, known as 'Tug', as, for some obscure reason, all Wilsons in the British Army are known. I remember his khaki uniform of thick coarse wool, impeccably tailored into riding breeches. He once put me on his great black charger and while nervous I was also delighted and my father took my picture with his small box camera. Sergeant Wilson had a fine physique, an upright military bearing, piercing blue eyes, a waxed moustache and a thundering voice. Altogether he was a fine figure of a man, the archetype of a British N.C.O.

I loved to drive around the military barracks of Tidworth for the street names read like a panorama of British history. Many of them were named after places in India, particularly those that figured in the Mutiny's holocaust – Lucknow, Meerut, Cawnpore. Many others were named after the bloody battles of the First World War – Ypres, Passchendaele and the Somme.

I got a different look at Tidworth in early February of 1944, for there it was that G.I. brides had to report for briefing and medical examinations before being transported to the States, courtesy of the United States Army. Here we sampled army life – the food plentiful but unappetizing served cafeteria style by German and Italian prisoners of war awaiting repatriation.

My last visit was in the summer of 1973, when my husband and I, in the company of his cousins Tom and Margaret McKnight, took a journey in which the men retraced the steps of their army careers. Tom had been stationed there in 1943 and 1944 and it was from Tidworth that he was able to journey to Marlborough and be present at our wedding. Tidworth in 1973 seemed an ordinary, drab military base – the magic of Tattoo night gone forever.

Though it was the First World War that most affected our lives when growing up, we were aware of previous wars that had in their turn made their mark on England.

One lady I knew, a Marlborough native who was a head teacher in Bath, had a great grandfather who had been a drummer boy at Waterloo in 1815.

One old man who had fought in the Crimean War (1854–1856) was still alive in Marlborough when I was a small child. There was a courtyard in the town known as Alma Place in honour of the Crimean battle of that name. Another local link with the Crimean War was in the person of the Earl of Cardigan, controversial and foolhardy leader of the ill-fated Charge of the Light Brigade at Balaclava. Perhaps he was the someone who had blundered. He was related to the Ailesburys and on his death without issue, his title passed to that family and became the title of the heir to the Marquess.

One of my father's very special soldier heroes was Lord Roberts. Short of stature and known to his men as 'Bobs', he was commander of the British Army in the Afghan wars in 1879. His most famous exploit was his forced march from Kabul to Kandahar in which he covered 313 miles in 23 days. The next day he relieved the latter city and soundly defeated an Afghan army which greatly outnumbered his men. Later he was in command during the South African War and was a leading proponent of general military training and service.

Many men a decade or so older than my parents, were veterans of the South African War (1899–1901). In 1914, many of these were called to the colours to fight once more in the war that was supposed to end all wars. We were told many times how in the South African War the bright red uniforms of the British soldiers were replaced with ones of khaki, a dusty yellowish brown which melted into the dun coloured veldt. Thus camouflaged the British were somewhat protected from the sharpshooting Boers.

CHAPTER XV

Yet one more factor that gave us a strong sense of heritage and history was the rule of monarchy. Both my parents felt the almost mystical reverence for royalty that was common in England and this they transmitted to us. They either turned a blind eye or brought an understanding heart to the sins, infidelities and foibles of Edward VII and his grandson the Prince of Wales, though the latter's abdication in 1936 less than a year after his succession as Edward VIII brought disillusionment to thousands and dealt the monarchy a severe blow. In fact it was saved only by the unbending dignity and uncompromising attitude of Queen Mary and the example of the succeeding king and his happy family life.

In school we prayed daily for the King and all the royal family and in church a beautiful prayer for their safekeeping was part of the liturgy. We sang loudly and often 'God Save the King' and 'God Bless the Prince of Wales.' We read avidly any item of royal news that came our way and we especially enjoyed rare glimpses of royalty's progress as it appeared in such publications at *The Illustrated London News*, The *Sphere* and The *Tatler*.

The first nationwide royal celebration that I can remember was the marriage of Princess Mary and Lord Lascelles, the heir to the Earl of Harewood. Princess Mary, later the Princess Royal, was the only daughter of King George V and Queen Mary and her Westminster Abbey wedding in 1922 was the occasion of a spectacle of pomp and circumstance unseen since before the War. Every town and village in England celebrated. In Marlborough a tea was given in the Town Hall for school children and we each received a souvenir mug on which were painted pictures of the bride and groom.

Another royal wedding took place some years later when Prince George, The Duke of Kent, took as his bride the beautiful Princess Marina of Greece. This event had a great influence on British fashion for Marina was a leader in style. Her favourite colour was a deep blue green named in her honour, Marina green, and it seemed as if every English girl and woman that year had a dress, blouse, coat or skirt in that delightful shade.

The birth of a daughter, Elizabeth, to the Duke and Duchess of York in 1926 was greeted with rejoicing. Four years later she was joined by a sister, Margaret Rose, who was born at her Scottish mother's ancestral home of Glamis Castle where much of the action in Shakespeare's play 'Macbeth' took place. These beautiful little girls captured the heart of England though few ever expected then, that the older would one day be a queen whose charm, dignity and strength of character have more than fulfilled her early promise.

King George V's Silver Jubilee took place in 1935 and great was the celebration all over England with church services, bonfires, dances, teas, dinners and all manner of festivities involving young and old. Such merrymaking helped take minds off the worsening conditions in Europe, but the joy was short lived for less than a year later the well loved monarch died. The nation was plunged into gloom and sadness. On the day of his funeral the nation en masse attended memorial services and listened to the wireless to the solemn obsequies in Westminster Abbey.

News of King George V's illness and death all but eclipsed the passing of Rudyard Kipling in the same week. But the poet who was the clarion voice of imperial British found his place of immortality in Westminster Abbey while his king and emperor was laid to rest in St. George's Chapel, Windsor. Though few realized it at the time, their deaths marked the end of an era.

All through the twenties the whole country hero-worshipped the boyish looking Prince of Wales. We followed his post-war progression around the world mending imperial fences and cementing ties
to the mother country. We admired him as he made visits to the depressed industrial areas of South Wales and northern England. We made excuses for his playboy propensities and many remained sympathetic to his involvement with Mrs. Simpson which ultimately led to his abdication.

When we were quite small children, we were taken to Swindon, eleven miles away, to see King George V and Queen Mary when they visited the Great Western Railway works. I was disappointed that I did not see them because of the tremendous crowds of people. I saw the present queen during the Second World War when she was serving in the A.T.S., and we often caught a glimpse of the Queen Mother, Mary as she drove from London to Badminton in the west country where she resided to escape the German bombing. She always rode sitting bolt upright in her ancient chauffeur driven maroon Daimler, wearing her familiar toque and favourite fox collared coats, bowing regally to admiring bystanders. She was the very embodiment of the unconquerable spirit of England.

Just as Princess Mary's wedding in 1922 had pierced the drabness of post-war depression, so the marriage of Princess Elizabeth in 1946 did the same in the dismal aftermath of World War II. But this time it was not merely the king's daughter marrying but the heir-presumptive to the throne. And her bridegroom was not an aging roué but a handsome, dashing naval officer of royal blood – Prince Philip of Greece, sailor nephew of British hero Lord Louis Mountbatten. It was indeed a fairy tale wedding.

On 12 March 1948, Marlborough had its own gala day when King George VI and Queen Elizabeth visited Marlborough College and were received at the Town Hall by the mayor and corporation. By that time, of course, I was in America.

There were other royal events that I watched on television in America, Princess Margaret's wedding to Anthony Armstrong-Jones, the investiture of Prince Charles as Prince of Wales, in Caernarvon Castle which we were able to visit the following year, and Princess Anne's wedding to Captain Phillips, son of a Wiltshire landowner.

1976 was Queen Elizabeth's Silver Jubilee. Again it was a time of rejoicing and early one June morning before going to my teaching job in Glen Rock, I watched on television, the service of Thanksgiving rendered in St. Paul's Cathedral in London. On that day, tea tables were set up in Marlborough's High Street, for the children of the town and they, in their turn, received mugs to commemorate the occasion.

On July 29th 1981 our alarm clock went off at 4 a.m. It was the day of the wedding of Prince Charles and Lady Diana Spencer and we were in a summer cottage on the coast of Maine which did not have a television set. But some old friends invited us to view the ceremony with them in their home some 30 miles away. And so it came about that we drove along the rain drenched country roads of Maine in the pre-dawn blackness to join people around the world to see the matchless spectacle of this fairy-tale wedding.

But of all royal events, it is the coronation of kings and queens that stresses the unbroken continuity, the history, the sanctity and the sacrament of monarchy. I remember the coronation of George VI, its magnificence and significance in no way dimmed by the older brother's abdication or the war clouds gathering over Europe. Twenty years later his daughter's coronation roused world-wide interest and once again reinforced the tie that binds people and sovereign. And this time because of television cameras in the Abbey itself, people were able to view the proceedings and participate as never before in the age-old ceremony that anointed and crowned as queen a slim young woman who would bear with honour and distinction the sacred trust which had come down to her through the centuries.

Royalty has given to England pomp, circumstance, pageantry, tradition and a sense of national unity, purpose and identity. Monarchy stabilizes a country, for governments come and governments go, but kingship goes on for ever – and when the king is dead, long lives the king.

Chapter XVI

Another relic of the past that we enjoyed in Marlborough, was our Town Crier. Important news was 'cried' at various stations throughout the town. He announced his presence by ringing a bell and shouting in stentorian tones 'Oyez! Oyez!' He then shouted out his message (usually incomprehensible to me when I was a child) and ended by raising his hat and bellowing forth 'God Save the King.' For many years our Town Crier was Mr. W.B. Angliss. Some of his children were school contemporaries of mine. Several times Mr. Angliss had won the national town crying championship competition which was held in Devonshire. He won both for the delivery and clarity of his pronouncements and for his costume. This was bright blue and consisted of velvet knee breeches and tail coat with white stockings, black silver buckled shoes, white lace stock and a black silk top hat. On special occasions the latter was replaced by a black tricorne. One of his stations used to be at the Seventh Wiltshire Regiments' memorial which was right outside our house and Mr. Angliss' arrival was always greeted with excitement and merited our close attention.

Chapter XVII

Food figured quite prominently in our childhood. Meals were always taken in the company of our parents, though my father was often absent because of his work. We had four meals a day – breakfast, dinner, tea and a light supper. My sister and I took turns to lay the table and clear the dishes away – the only domestic obligations laid upon us.

For breakfast we had either eggs or porridge. The eggs were sometimes served with bacon. Mother liked bacon that was imported from Denmark even though the county of Wiltshire was famous for its local pig products. This preference cost her dearly but she never deviated from it until the war prevented imports from reaching England and bacon was rationed. The rashers were cut from the back portion of the pig. Eggs – brown ones were preferred – were often boiled and served to us in our own egg cups, being eaten out of the shell with a small spoon and strips of bread and butter. Sunday mornings brought the special treat of scrambled or, as we knew them, buttered eggs, served on toast. Marmalade, jam both generally homemade, and, of course, the inevitable honey were always present on the breakfast table. Porridge or oatmeal was served with brown, or demarara sugar and hot milk and was a substitute for eggs during the winter months. We were told that it would stick to our ribs and help ward off the cold. Occasionally we had kippers but the many bones took away the pleasure and we vastly preferred smoked haddock cooked in a delicate sauce of butter and milk. Grilled kidneys were another rare treat. Except for an occasional serving of prunes, no fruit or juice appeared at breakfast.

Our main meal was at midday, ready when we came in from school. When Father was out his dinner was put aside for reheating. Certain meal routines were predictable. On Sunday we always had a roast – by turns beef, lamb, pork or veal. On Monday, we had the leftover meat served cold. It was wash day – Mother's temper was often short and Monday's dinner was not up to her usual standard. On Tuesday, she made the remains of Sunday's roast into a savoury dish such as Shepherd's pie, or Lancashire hot pot. For the rest of the week, the meals could not be predicted. Very often a delicious odour as we entered the house would tell us what was for dinner. Sometimes, it was steak and kidney pie or pudding (one baked, the other steamed), or it might be rabbit, tripe and onions, liver, stuffed heart or fish. Roast chicken was a rare treat and turkey (not at all like the broad breasted birds of today) came but once a year at Christmas. My mother took great pains with her cooking and she always made the correct sauces that, were considered the proper accompaniment to certain dishes – mint sauce with lamb, Yorkshire pudding and horseradish sauce with roast beef, hot apple sauce and crackling with pork, red currant jelly with veal and game, and bread sauce and forcemeat or sage and onion stuffing with poultry. Chestnut stuffing was added to the Christmas turkey. Boiled potatoes were standard fare at every meal, even when potatoes cooked in other ways were served. A great variety of vegetables appeared in summer but in winter they dwindled down to cabbage and brussel sprouts and root vegetables like turnips and parsnips. Salad was served only in summer and only with cold meat or tinned salmon. The pudding that followed the meat course was a very important part of the meal and was often a very filling dish. Mother was a fine hand at pastry making and whenever fruit was available she made pies. Every scrap of pastry was used to make jam turnovers which usually went into my father's lunch package. We liked boiled suet puddings served with golden syrup, treacle tarts and apple charlotte and in summer enjoyed the junkets, custards and blancmanges that went with stewed fruit. I did not like rice pudding then, though now I often make it in the creamy English style for my husband and myself. Tapioca pudding I detested, the slimy tapioca reminding me of frog spawn, but I learned to swallow it without complaining as Mother would brook no nonsense at meal times. The famous English dessert trifle was reserved for party occasions as it was expensive to make.

Tea was always ready when we got home from school something after four o'clock. There was thin bread and butter – Mother prided herself that she always served butter and never margarine – to be spread with jam or Shippham's meat or fish paste and followed by cake. Mother made a cake every week – a plain un-iced no nonsense cake. Sometimes it was Madeira cake (absolutely plain, so called because it was commonly served in gentry's houses with Madeira wine), sometimes sultana, currant, cherry or carraway seed cake, which were all variations of the basic Madeira cake. I did not like seed cake. The seeds stuck in my teeth and their pungent taste burned my tongue. Sometimes she made a very special kind of ginger cake which we loved. I always cut the top off to eat it last it was so delicious. When her homemade cake was eaten she resorted to the bakery to buy some of the confections for which Wiltshire was famous – lard cake, dough cake and a variety of buns and doughnuts. The lard cake served warm melted in one's mouth and I early acquired a taste for dough cake, sad, heavy and loaded with fruit. Of the buns I liked Chelsea buns for they could be unwound into a long strip of sugary dough. Sunday tea was very special – salad, canned meat and fish was served, jelly (jello) with fruit added to it and a variety of sweet cakes and biscuits. Lyons, the great London restaurant chain, used to put out many kinds of boxed cakes and their cream sandwich cakes were a regular feature of our Sunday tea for many years. Sunday was the day and tea was the meal for enter-taining and unless we ourselves were out visiting, rarely a Sunday went by without company for tea. Our teachers were often invited and other family friends. During the week Mother's friends might occasionally pop in (there was no telephone for advance notice) and stay for tea and then there would be the challenge of providing for guests something more than the usual bread and butter and plain cake. In the winter, we often had buttered toast made with a long handled brass toasting fork over an open fire or on special occasions crumpets, those sad, heavy, damp rounds of dough toasted till brown and buttered so lavishly that their holes dripped with the golden molten grease. When I first came to New York, Cushman's, the now defunct cake chain, occasionaly sold crumpets but now I have not seen them for years, in England no less than in the United States. Muffins in my earliest memory were brought around by a man carrying a bag of them atop his head. He rang a bell to announce his coming. The muffins were split, toasted and buttered for tea. One of the greatest treats of childhood was to be taken out to tea in a restaurant. Tea was the culmination of a day's outing in such towns as Bath, Salisbury, Swindon or Oxford. Bread and butter, jam, toasted tea cakes were followed by a choice of cream cakes.

One real English tea I remember, was served by my Aunt May in her tiny cottage in Ford, Wiltshire in 1954 when, we as a family, made our first trip back to England. She had the most wonderful spread – salad, sandwiches, cold meat and fish, jellies, custards, bread and butter, jam, cakes, and biscuits of all kinds. My husband and I have never forgotten that tea and hope our boys, then six and three, have some memory of it.

In July 1983 we had another English Sunday tea at my niece Rachel's home in Weymouth. We had some American friends with us who enjoyed it too.

Tea for us, as children was really the last meal of the day but before bedtime, we had a snack, usually bread and cheese and biscuits with milk, lemonade or hot cocoa to drink according to the season.

Chapter XVIII

Certain seasons brought about a real flurry of activity in the kitchen. Christmas was the most important of these, with Easter, a close second.

Preparation for Christmas cakes, plum puddings and mincemeat began in October, when ingredients such as dried fruit and candied peel poured in to the food shops in quantity. The round fruit cakes, one large and two medium size, were made first and stored in big tins till they were iced just before Christmas. Until then each cake received a weekly tablespoonful or so of brandy poured over it partly to preserve it and partly to give it flavour. Though we rarely had any liquor in the house – my father was a teetotaller – Mother always bought a bottle of Martell's five star brandy in October to see us through the Christmas season. Most of it was used in the puddings, cakes and mincemeat and any left over was kept for medicinal purposes.

When the time came for the cakes to be iced they were done not once but twice. First came a thick layer of almond paste or marzipan made from egg yolks, sugar and finely ground almonds. The latter were a standard item of fare around holiday time in British grocery stores and I was surprised to find they were well nigh unobtainable here and that icing of any kind was not used on fruit cake in the States. Then on top of the almond paste went a stiff, hard, white frosting known as Royal icing made of confectioners' sugar and egg whites. The Royal icing could be piped through a bag and tube to form rosettes for decoration and the words 'Merry Christmas' were often written on top of the cake in icing made pink with cochineal. It was necessary to work very fast with Royal icing or it hardened too much. Mother was always very tense and nervous when icing the cakes. Finally the cake was surrounded with a fancy paper frill. On one of the smaller cakes May and I were permitted to make a snow scene, roughing the white icing up into hills on which miniature trees grew or down which Father Christmas came coasting in his sleigh drawn by reindeer. Sometimes Mother would buy crystallized violets and rose petals for decoration, sometimes small marzipan fruits and always an ounce of silver balls, hard, shiny pellets which when crunched had a faint flavour of peppermint. We bought all our cake decorations from a shop called Irving's which was on the corner of the High Street, as it curved and climbed into Kingsbury Street. One entered this small store up three rounded, time-worn steps through a double door with frosted glass panels. The shop was crammed from floor to ceiling with fancy grocery items, biscuits, confectionery and all kinds of Christmas fare. The most marvellous cake decorations could be found there, many of them imported from Germany, Holland or France. It was a veritable old curiosity shop of holiday food specialities – its wares and smells enchanted me and we spent magic minutes there making agonizing decisions while Mother anxiously counted out pennies from the worn crocodile purse trimmed with silver, which my father had given her years before and which she used until it literally fell apart.

After the cakes were made she concentrated on the mincemeat which she made in considerable quantity. May and I were pressed into service to help with the stoning of raisins, chopping of candied peel and suet. For our efforts we were rewarded with the lumps of hard sugar that came out of the candied lemon, orange, or citron halves that we had to cut up. Currants, light and dark sultanas (stoneless raisins) and huge raisins complete with pips all had to be washed, dried, have stems removed and the stones taken out, tedious, time-consuming work. Mother used to make dozens of small mincepies in the weeks before Christmas and any errand boy, tradesman, or postman who called was offered one. They melted in the mouth and her mincepies became quite famous. While I make a good large mincepie, I cannot begin to duplicate her small ones.

But by far the most important part of the Christmas preparations, was the making of the puddings. All the prepared fruit, breadcrumbs and other dry ingredients were assembled the night before in an enormous brown pottery crock used only for making the puddings. Before we went to school that morning, we had to stir a wish into the mixture as Mother added beer, brandy and a dozen eggs. Last of all was added new silver money obtained from the bank for that express purpose and tiny silver charms which would surface in the Christmas Day servings of the puddings. Finding a ring meant a wedding, a thimble doomed a girl to spinsterhood and a button for a boy indicated the life of a carefree bachelor. What fun it all was! After standing in the crock for twenty-four hours, the pudding mixture was finally put into buttered basins, tied up with paper and cloth and steamed or boiled for several hours in the copper with the fire underneath, where Monday's wash was always done. When we came home from school the very distinct smell of boiling puddings greeted us and sometimes we were treated to a small pudding made from the scrapings of the bowl.

My mother was just as nervous about the puddings as Mrs. Cratchit – in fact, I can never read Dickens' account of Cratchits' Christmas dinner without a lump in the throat so closely did he catch the very essence of the Christmas dinner of a humble English family. When the pudding was brought in wreathed in the blue flames of ignited brandy with a sprig of holly crowning it, that moment indeed, seemed the culmination and distillation of the spirit of Christmas Day.

January was marmalade making time. The Seville oranges from Spain came into the stores right after Christmas. Too sour and bitter to eat as fruit they all went into marmalade which was, and still is, a staple of the British breakfast. Again May and I were coerced to cut up peel and pulp and stir the boiling mass of fruit and sugar. Once Mother made some grapefruit marmalade. We had tried grapefruit but did not like its bitter sourness. All England's citrus fruit was imported from the Mediterranean countries and our favourite oranges were the oval thick skinned Jaffas from Palestine. I still think they are second to none even in this land of the California and Florida fruit.

February brought the very special treat of pancakes on Shrove Tuesday. The pancakes were thin brown and crisp and always served sprinkled with sugar and lemon juice. In the Lenten weeks that followed, meals became plainer and simpler with boiled fish, usually cod, with egg sauce served every Friday. On Good Friday, we ate Hot Cross Buns and the final boiled fish dinner. Roast lamb was traditional for Easter Day dinner and, of course, we ate hard boiled eggs and enjoyed a wide variety of candy and chocolate eggs. In addition, Mother always made what she called Easter cakes, flat round biscuits with currants in them and sugar sprinkled on top.

Summer's abundance of fruit and vegetables caused a hectic period of jam, jelly and pickle making and Mother often made enough to last most of the year. We took gooseberry, raspberry, strawberry and plum jam very much for granted but waxed enthusiastic about black currant, red currant and damson. In early October, we all used to go blackberrying and when we were successful Mother made blackberry jelly, as well as the most delicious blackberry and apple pies.

When there was illness in the house Mother would feed her patient special food. She would buy shin of beef, scrape it and cook it for hours to make beef tea. Baked egg custards were fed to invalids as well as jellies and milk puddings, and lightly boiled eggs.

In addition to feeding us well on her very limited budget, Mother believed in dietary supplements and patent medicines. At various times we were subjected to Scott's Emulsion, thick, creamy white and tasting of fish, malt and codliver oil, sweetly viscous in a big brown jar and Parrish's food, a thin red liquid containing iron which we drank, diluted with water, from a wine glass. Following a cold or flu we were 'built up' with bedtime cups of Horlick's Malted Milk, chocolate flavoured Ovaltine or Bovril, a salty beef essence stirred into boiling water. When laxatives were needed, Mother relied on California Syrup of Figs. She had great faith in this, crediting it with saving my sister's life when she was a very small child. I disliked this particular medicine more than any other, even Scott's Emulsion. Once to her horror Mother discovered we had worms and I remember very clearly how I hated the chocolate tablets sprinkled with coloured candy that contained the medicine for this particular affliction. Fortunately it effected a cure very quickly.

My Father, Joseph Frank Biggs, as a young man, about 1904

My Father in chauffeur uniform

The pre-war cars my father drove

Mrs Hume, my mother's employer before my parents' marriage in 1911

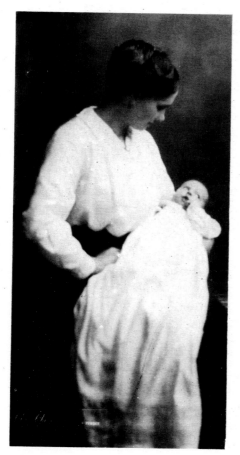

My mother with my sister May after the baby's christening in early 1916

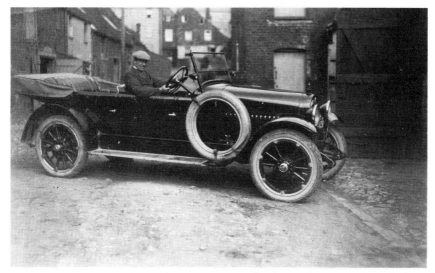

My father in the Hudson touring car he drove for Mr. Hooper

Our family taken in 1918

Wearing hand knitted dresses in 1921

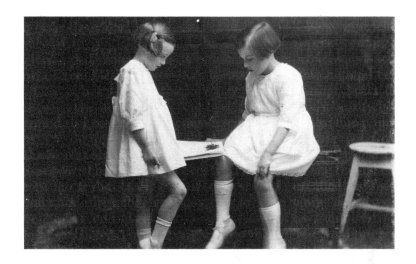

Above: White silk dresses for Whitsun

Right: 'Jack and Jill' at a church fete

Class at St. Mary's Girls' School Marlborough in 1925. I am 3rd from left in top row

Chapter XIX

Food, its preparation, its seasonal joys and delights, the partaking of meals by the whole family, is very important to a growing child. We enjoyed being with our parents, listening to their conversation and often contributing to it while we ate the food so lovingly prepared and so often concocted out of very little.

My mother rarely purchased food directly from a shop. Rather she wrote out orders, some weekly, some daily, which we, as school-children, took to the grocer and the butcher. The goods were brought to the house by an errand boy or delivery man. Bread and milk were delivered to the house regularly. Milk was ladled into the pint or quart jugs left on the doorstep, from a tin can. No one in those days seemed concerned about germs. When I was very small, all the tradesmen used horse-drawn vehicles but the twenties brought about a change to mechanized vans. The tradespeople became good friends who always had time for a short chat. They were quite important in my mother's rather lonely life. To some extent we shared their joys and tragedies, as they did ours.

Lovely brown eggs were bought from an elderly gentleman, named Mr. Bassett, who parked his car in certain places and then called on his customers with his eggs in a big basket. He had a large purple veined nose, steel-rimmed spectacles and a very prim and precise way of speaking over-emphasizing his consonants. May and I would sometimes mimic him, though not in Mother's hearing. She was most particular about our showing all due respect to our elders and was always very considerate of people's feelings. Mr. Bassett also interested us because of his religion – he was a member of the sect known as the Plymouth Brethren and was known on occasions to utter a little prayer during his egg transactions. This religious group was talked about quite a bit by my parents. The members met in a rented room not far from us until, growing rapidly, they had to seek larger quarters. A good friend of ours joined this sect after the birth of her second child who, unfortunately, was retarded. This poor little girl was a source of much curiosity and concern and we were all relieved when she died at an early age. But her mother and older sister remained devoted adherents of the little church which had supported them spiritually through their ordeal.

The grocer we traded with was a fat genial redheaded man. He was a leading citizen in the town and a pillar of the Methodist church. He would always give me a biscuit or a sweet but as I got older a pat on the behind or a squeeze around the waist was added to his other favours. Mother would have been horrified so I never told her but became adept at evading his attentions.

Additional bread, cakes and buns were bought from a shop next door to the grocer. It was operated by two old maids who became friends of Mother's and took a considerable interest in the two of us, rather engaging little girls always dressed tastefully and often alike. We could always count on an extra cake or biscuit and were sometimes invited to take tea in the rooms behind the shop. These were elegantly furnished on our standards and we liked going there very much for a marvellous spread always awaited us. These two ladies attended my wedding and I wrote to them until they died.

The butcher we traded with lived a few yards up the road from us. He had a large family of children some of whom were in school with us. The floor of his little shop was covered in sawdust, often blood spattered and outside the shop were hung rabbits, pheasants and poultry with fur and feathers still on. Mother could skin a rabbit very quickly and pluck a chicken too but she would never permit us to watch her doing so. It was, of course, cheaper to buy rabbits and birds undressed. Travelling around the farms in his work, Father was sometimes given rabbits or an occasional chicken, pheasant, partridge or joint of venison. I remember once, we were inundated with pigeons or squabs and grew tired of them, in spite of the various ways Mother presented them. Rabbits we liked very much especially when they were baked covered in buttered crumbs and herbs. We liked the kidneys and they were always divided between us. Such gifts certainly helped the budget and added variety to our menus.

Mother supplemented her weekly grocery delivery by purchases from the small general shops that sprang up on many a corner. Most of these purchases were made by May or myself. Moonraker brand butter, a local product, was always bought from Pond's, just a few yards up the road and we often ran across the road to the general store that stood there for a can of soup, baked beans, a jar of pickles or a bottle of 'Daddy's' sauce. The proprietors of these two stores became good friends over the years. These stores were open early and did not close until late – they were open holiday times but closed on Sundays in keeping with the religious feeling of the times.

When we were small and going to St. Mary's School, my mother would often meet us out of school at four in the afternoon. The school was about one-half mile from home and the way led uphill through the pretty area of the town known as the Green – two large expanses of green bisected by the Swindon road and an avenue of lime trees leading to St. Mary's Church. The mothers enjoyed talking as they waited at the bottom of the school steps for the children to come out. But as we grew older Mother went out less and less. Some weeks it was only Saturdays that she went into the town.

For many years I accompanied her on this weekly peregrination and we would walk the full length of the top side of the High Street returning along the lower side – the wide street had a distinct slope from north to south. We commonly referred to the top and bottom sides of the High Street and I remember how this terminology confused the Americans in World War II. Occasionally we stopped at one of the shops for a modest purchase – perhaps one-half pint of cream from the dairy or some knitting wool in a shop kept by two elderly ladies named Miss Trehearne and Miss Lawrence. The many colours of the different varieties of wool fascinated me as a child, and for some forgotton reason, I was always disappointed if gray-haired Miss Lawrence waited on us instead of plump Miss Trehearne whose pince nez were always falling off her nose.

Sometimes the round trip took a long while depending on the weather, the number of our errands and the number of people we met with whom we stopped and chatted. There was one old lady who was very deaf whom I hated to meet and on some occasions my mother was known to hastily cross the street to avoid her. If I grew impatient with the adult talk I would be sharply told to be quiet. If it was wet we scurried quickly along the top side of the street where there was a partial penthouse built for protection against the rain.

Chapter XX

As a child our year was broken into three very distinct segments as determined by the school terms. Except for the beginning and end of the school year, its divisions were dictated by festivals of the Christian Church. The school year started in September and ran until Christmas when there was a longish holiday of two to three weeks. The spring term ran until Easter, again the time of a rather lengthy break after which it continued until mid-July. There was, however, a week's holiday at Whitsun, the old English name for the ecclesiastical feast of Pentecost and there was a half-term break in late October. Holidays tended to be longer at the Grammar School than at St. Mary's.

Christmas, of course, was the biggest holiday of all, though Boxing Day on 26 December was a public holiday too, and almost as important as Christmas Day itself. I think it is a very necessary holiday if only for recovery purposes and I was shocked to find it not celebrated in the United States. The tradition of Boxing Day, it is believed, arose during the Victorian era when the leftovers from the Christmas feasts of the wealthy were boxed up and distributed to the poor and needy. In Marlborough, Boxing Day became the time when boxing contests among the lads from the nearby racing stables were held, which as a child gave me an alternative though of course mistaken reason for the name.

We always spent Christmas Day at home generally just the four of us. After a special breakfast of ham and eggs, presents were opened. Mother had laid them out on the sofa in the sitting room – we had already found our stockings full of small gifts hanging on the bedpost when we awoke. We had roast turkey and all the trimmings for dinner, the bird being a present from my father's employer and then a high tea about six with all manner of goodies. As a small child the Christmas I remember best was the one when I woke up with mumps. Mother quietly cleared the presents off the sofa and installed me there for the day in front of a roaring fire. The attention I got more than compensated me for my fat face and its attendant discomfort. It became the custom to spend Boxing Day with our close friends, the Garsides and their three boys who were somewhat younger than we were. The Garsides always had a Christmas tree (which we did not) for the stocking was the vehicle for gifts for most English children at that time. The tree had been introduced into England from Germany by Queen Victoria's husband, Prince Albert, but since most trees had to be imported the cost was prohibitive for many people and the tree's Teutonic origin tended to make it somewhat unpopular in the years following the First World War.

We always had a lot of fun on Boxing Day eating cold ham, turkey and beef, cold Christmas pudding, mince pies and sherry trifle. We crowded with the other guests into their small house, at the end gathering around the piano and singing carols and World War I songs with an enthusiasm that made up for the occasional wrong notes. I waited for "A Long Long Trail A-Winding" to be sung. Its sentimentality made my eyes prick and my throat constrict.

Mr. Garside, who worked in the office of the auctioneer who employed my father, was a slim quiet gentle man, in appearance almost a double for the Duke of York who later became George VI. Mrs. Garside who came from Grantham in Lincolnshire and had an accent quite distinct from the Wiltshire dialect we were used to, was plump and jolly. They had met in a canteen during the war. Mr. Garside had joined up as a very young man, was wounded twice and had received the Distinguished Conduct Medal for gallantry in the field, making him the most highly decorated ex-soldier in Marlborough. He was very quiet and gentle and had a fine mind and a strict sense of duty. He eventually became a partner in the auctioneering business, was quite successful and was active in many facets of town life. He was a loyal member of the British Legion and a strong supporter of the local Conservative Party and because of his wife, to whom he was devoted, a faithful Wesleyan. After my parents had died the Garsides became even more dear to me. It was a great pleasure when they visited us in Glen Rock in 1961 and we never went to Marlborough without seeing them and visiting them in their lovely home in Hyde Lane which had succeeded the tiny council house where we had had so much Boxing Day fun. Mrs. Garside died first, breaking his heart, but he continued to live on in the house with two of his sons for several more years. We spent a lovely day with him in 1972 going to Bath and Longleat House but the following Spring he succumbed to a stroke. I remain in touch with Phil, the oldest son who was closest to me in age.

Easter was second in importance to Christmas and was a joyful occasion celebrated with eggs, real ones dyed and decorated, chocolate ones, baskets and new clothes, but no Easter bunny. It was preceded by the sadness and gloom of Good Friday when long church services, Hot Cross Buns, boiled cod, potatoes and egg sauce were the order of the day.

On Whitsunday (corruption of White Sunday), which came six weeks after Easter and marked the descent of the Holy Ghost, we wore white dresses when we went to Church. They were symbolic of the pureness of hearts ready to receive the Holy Spirit. This custom gradually faded out during my childhood years and Whitsun was the first religious holiday to fall victim to the wave of materialism and secularism which swept Britain in the 1920s and 1930s. Both Easter Monday and Whit Monday were bank holidays – public holidays in American parlance – thus creating long weekends. Easter was also expanded by Good Friday. During those years weekend road traffic was to grow increasingly heavy until war-time petrol rationing caused all but the military and essential traffic to disappear from the highways. Prior to the war it was the custom for many poorer families to use their car only during the summer. This saved considerably on auto taxation as well as petrol which was always quite expensive in England as, until the recent discovery of North Sea oil, it had to be imported. The custom too of taxing vehicles according to horsepower and number of wheels gave rise to many small cars such as the Baby Austin, Morris Minor, as well as the three-wheel Morgan and it also popularized the motor bike. When I was young, a car was used principally for pleasure and daily or regular transportation was provided by bicycle, motor bicycle and an excellent bus service which linked every little town with its network of villages. In addition train service was good. Many of the Grammar School pupils who came in from outlying villages rode the regular buses and trains.

The first Monday in August, the traditional holiday month in England, was a bank holiday which meant a long weekend in high summer. Chosen originally because of the greater likelihood of good weather, the date has now been moved to the last Monday in August and marks the official end of summer, as Labor Day does in the United States.

Most people tried to take one or two weeks at the seaside during the summer, staying in boarding houses and praying for good weather. It was a mark of our poverty that we were never able to afford such a holiday. May and I felt deprived and embarrassed by this. During the summer, however, Mother would arrange for us, alone or together, to visit friends and relations and I remember some enjoyable holidays with my aunts May and Nellie and with friends at various times. We stayed in Potterne and Urchfont, villages near Devizes, in Salisbury, Wiltshire's cathedral town, and with an uncle who lived in Hampstead in northwest London. Such visits were high spots in our childhood. In addition, we took several day trips to the seaside every year. Bournemouth and Weymouth were the most accessible but Father's favourites were Canford Cliffs in Hampshire and Minehead in Somerset. I well remember the anxious scanning of the skies, the early starts and the picnic basket which among other delectables always carried the rare treat of potted tongue.

There were other holidays to punctuate the year, some of national and some of regional significance. Some of them are now nothing but anachronisms, mere relics of the past and probably now scarcely heard of and no longer celebrated. Empire Day (May 24) and Queen Victoria's birthday, St. George's Day (April 23) which was also Shakespeare's birthday, and Trafalgar Day (October 21) are three which come to mind. They were marked with a whole or half day off from school and preceded by lessons which established their relevance and importance in our minds. Guy Fawkes Day (November 5), the anniversary of the unsuccessful Gunpowder Plot to blow up the Houses of Parliament in 1605, was marked by town fireworks and an enormous bonfire on the Common where an effigy of Guy was burned. The assembled crowd would join hands around the fire and chant:

> Remember remember
> The 5th of November
> Gunpowder treason and plot.

The acrid air made our noses and eyes sting and Mother disliked Guy Fawkes Day saying we always caught colds. Years later I was to feel the same about the Halloween wanderings of my two boys.

Armistice Day (November 11) was a very solemn day in school. Marking the end of the First World War it was not a holiday but an occasion when we sang sad songs, wore Lord Haig's red poppies, kept the two-minute silence (I always dreaded that I would sneeze, cough or otherwise disgrace myself in that short space of time that seemed interminable). One hymn we never sang in those days was "Glorious Things of Thee Are Spoken." Being the German national anthem the hurt and scars left by the war were still too raw.

And so the years of childhood went by – slowly then it seemed – in retrospect all too fast.

Chapter XXI

We were not a regular churchgoing family. My father had long considered himself an agnostic but Mother, true to her Anglican upbringing, saw that we attended St. Mary's Sunday School and always took us to church services at Christmas, Easter and Whitsun. Sunday School seemed largely to consist of memorization of Biblical verses and as a reward for mastery or effort we were presented with 'texts' which we commonly mispronounced as 'texes'. These were small stiff shiny cards with a garish coloured picture of religious import with a verse from the Bible printed underneath. I soon acquired a big collection of these and going over them gave me much pleasure. The best parts of Sunday School were the Christmas Party and the summer outing. The latter meant an all-day bus (we called it a charabanc) trip to a seaside resort, usually Bournemouth, Weymouth, or Weston-super-Mare and the former was a big tea served in the church hall with sandwiches, cakes, jellies, blancmange and biscuits, followed by games and gifts from the Christmas tree. We always got an orange, an apple, some sweets and occasionally a little book or toy and sometimes these gifts were packaged in a little net stocking with the local rector playing 'Father Christmas'. At the end of the Sunday School year prizes were given for good attendance and the year sometimes ended with a picnic at Bradenoak in Savernake Forest.

Sometimes in the summer Mother used to take us to Evensong at one of the two town churches or more excitingly to our parish church of Preshute. This was a tiny Norman church on the banks of the river and on the western outskirts of the town, and the fact that we were in Preshute parish was an anomaly due to ecclesiastical boundaries dating from medieval times. Going to Preshute entailed a two-mile walk through the water meadows of the River Kennet in the shadow of Granham Hill, a spur on the downs bearing one of the famous Wiltshire White Horses. The short turf had been removed in the shape of a horse, exposing the white chalk underneath. After service was over we usually walked back through the town where Mother would sometimes stop to chat with any friends she might meet.

Though we went to church rather haphazardly we were prepared for confirmation in our early teens and in due course, dressed all in white, we went to the service at which the Bishop of Salisbury laid his hands on us and made us full communicant members of the Church of England.

Mother was proud of her Church of England affiliation and I am sure she felt superior to members of the Nonconformist churches whom she designated by the all-inclusive term 'chapel' as opposed to 'church'. When I became engaged to Lieutenant David Wharton of the United States Army I was glad to be able to tell Mother that my husband-to-be was a Presbyterian. In 1944 the Church of Scotland was practically unheard of in rural Southern England and Mother's comment was "Well, at least I am glad he is not 'chapel'."

We were, however, relatively well-informed in Biblical matters for in all English schools religious instruction was compulsory. Many of the elementary schools of my day were 'church' schools including the one I attended. This meant they were partially supported by the Church of England which assumed responsibility for and exercised some control over the religious education of pupils. In the church schools, church history, dogma and doctrine were taught in addition to the Biblical knowledge compulsory in all schools. Doctrine was taught, at least to certain of the older classes, by the local rector or vicar usually on a weekly basis and this duty was generally taken rather seriously and performed conscientiously.

The daily religious instructional period usually lasted for thirty minutes and followed the morning assembly of the entire school which consisted of hymns, prayers and a short sermon or homily by the headmaster or mistress. Of the instructional periods two were devoted to Old Testament study, two to the new Testament, while the fifth day was reserved for doctrine and church history in the church schools and used as a time for revision and testing in the other state schools. Both Old and New Testaments were taught as literature and/or history and pains were taken to keep us chronologically and geographically in line and a set syllabus was strictly adhered to. We were exposed to the beautiful language of the King James' Version of the Bible and the map of the Holy Land (Palestine as it was then known) became almost as familiar to us as the map of England.

I also learned a little about Christian Science from my mother. She had been given a copy of the Christian Science Handbook by her employer, Mr. Hume, when he turned to Christian Science after regular medical treatment had failed him. Mother spoke of Mary Baker Eddy and Boston, Massachusetts. While Mother realised the healing power of faith, she was always quick to call the doctor in when any of her family fell ill.

During the twenties, many English people turned to the new 'science' of spiritualism for help and comfort in those depressed days – perhaps in a vain effort to establish contact with the youthful dead in the First World War. I heard Mother and Dad talk of mediums and séances and Sir Oliver Lodge's name was often mentioned. I can still recall newspaper pictures of the burly octogenarian with the shock of white hair.

Another religious idol of Mother's was the Reverend Dick Shepherd of St. Martin's-in-the-Fields. A popular padre in the twenties, he became a noted preacher and writer. His articles appeared in the *Sunday Express* and Mother read them avidly. He died of cancer in his forties, writing of his approaching death during his illness. A few years ago, Dr. Melvin Campbell, quoted Dick Shepherd at great length in one of his sermons in the West Side Presbyterian Church in Ridgewood, New Jersey.

Chapter XXII

The most traumatic experience in my young life was my bout with scarlet fever. Contracted at the age of five, less than a week after I started school, I had to endure a long stay in the isolation hospital. This was a large forbidding building of grey stone surrounded by a high wall and stood north of the town on the edge of a wide flat grassy area known as the Common.

The hospital had originally been the workhouse or poor house – the thought of ultimately going there had haunted the indigent and elderly for generations. The exposure of the evil squalor in Dickens' books had done much to eliminate or improve such institutions. When the Marlborough workhouse was closed, the buildings with some minimal renovations were converted into the isolation hospital. Years later, as the diseases which had kept it filled were brought under control, it was used, cheerless as it was, as a children's convalescent home. Next to it – hopefully the location purely coincidental – was the town cemetery.

I was in a children's ward filled to overflowing for the disease was epidemic. Highly contagious as it was, no visitors were allowed.

I had literally been torn from my mother's arms by Mr. Lloyd, the hospital superintendent who picked me up in a horse-drawn vehicle. He was a fat little man with a long body and very short legs. His face was round and cherubic and he wore pebble glasses that shone and accentuated the roundness of his face. I was in an agony of fear and apprehension, but he was kind and gentle, far more so than his wife who was the matron of the hospital. She was dressed in a stiff starched uniform, was very strict and to me appeared totally devoid of sympathy or understanding. My first meal was bread and milk which I refused, whereupon she forcibly fed me, and slapped me when I vomited. Food was bare subsistence fare and families who could afford to do so used to supplement it by bringing eggs, butter, fruit, cake and other luxuries up to the hospital. Such things were shared by all. My mother faithfully brought her contributions. Among them, one day, was a Victoria sponge spread with strawberry jam, for many years my favourite cake. When Matron cut it she miscounted for there turned out to be one less slice than there were patients. Naturally, I was the one who went without. This was quite a bitter pill for a sheltered and relatively indulged five-year-old to swallow. In fact, my memories of the isolation hospital to this day hold a Dickensian quality of overcrowding, poor food and small acts of unfairness.

After six weeks I was released, but shortly thereafter suffered a relapse. I infected my sister and my father who had to go to the hospital, but I remained at home under Mother's care. I developed very swollen glands in my neck and it was only my mother's good around-the-clock nursing that saved me from the disfiguring scars that the operation to relieve them left. I remember the application of hot cotton wool that she used to apply every couple of hours day and night. She used to bake the cotton in a round cake tin. She was exhausted with nursing me and extremely worried about my sister and especially my father who developed the serious complication of erysipelas. Mother was a natural nurse. Much of her skill was innate but she had learned much fom her own mother caring for her numerous younger brothers and sisters. Though illness was dreaded, it presented a challenge which brought out the best in her. At one time both my sister and I were operated on for abscessed ears at home, my mother preparing her bedroom as a surgery and assisting the doctor, following his directions as best she could. I can still smell the sickly sweet odour of the choloroform.

The one illness that really frightened Mother was appendicitis. She had lost her father and her older sister with it – and came close to losing her husband. She viewed any stomach ache with dread and suspicion. She was white with fear and anxiety when she was summoned by telephone to Putney Hospital whither I had been rushed in the middle of one night from the London College I attended. She had difficulty in reconciling her preconceived idea of appendicitis with the normal and rather speedy recovery I made.

During the weeks of illness following my discharge from the isolation hospital my mother and I were completely alone. I feel that it was then that the very close relationship I had with my mother first began to develop. She told me stories of her childhood which I never tired of hearing, read to me and played with me. Our closeness lasted all her life, even though after the age of eighteen I never lived at home for very long. Distance was bridged by letters. Hers came twice a week. For many years a dark red three halfpenny stamp was affixed to the inside of every letter to guarantee a reply, but I found it as rewarding to answer her letters as to receive them. Her loss in 1946, just as I had commenced a new life in America, was a bitter blow.

Chapter XXIII

As a child I lived very much in the world of the imagination. I used to daydream a lot and sometimes could not wait to go to bed so that I could enjoy my fantasy land undisturbed.

I wanted desperately to go abroad. Drawing on my reading and knowledge of geography, and in envy of friends with Indian or colonial backgrounds or connections, I spent many imaginary hours in 'foreign parts'. Insular as we were, we were quite used to hearing of young men going out to India and young women going as brides to share their husbands' fortunes in the colonies and the very names of places like Burma, Singapore and British Guiana conjured up all kinds of romantic notions. Of all places, I dreamed most of going to Rhodesia. I had read and enjoyed Olive Schreiner's *Tales of an African Farm* and the chequered career of Cecil Rhodes fascinated me. Many years later, my husband made several business trips to Rhodesia and found it as delightful a country as my imagination had led me to suppose. But I never accompanied him there and as the political situation changed so his business connections ceased. It seems odd to me after over thirty-five years of living here that never once did I think of the United States as an imaginary escape hatch.

At one time, probably when we were about nine and eleven respectively, my sister and I entered into a serialized imaginary adventure together always referred to as 'that game'. Our conversational adventures as an Irish peer's daughter (me) and an English girl of aristocratic family (May), who met at boarding school, were carried on sotto voce in nightly dialogues until they were terminated by sleep or parents' threats to be quiet. My sister, more prosaic than I, older and more sophisticated, never entered into the spirit of the game as fully as I did nor did she contribute as much imaginatively. After playing enthusiastically for some weeks she began to bribe me to do things for her in return for participation in 'that game'. May and I shared a room and a double bed and while I believe that, ideally, every child should have his or her own room, yet we enjoyed for many years a closeness and companionship that otherwise would have been lost to us. Now that she is dead, and remembering that her long illness and my living so far away prevented us from getting together very often in adult life, I cherish the memory of our childhood nights together, when our daylight differences seemed to disappear and we were at peace with each other.

Boarding school figured quite prominently in my imaginary reveries. It seemed to have a special cachet, probably because for economic reasons it was unattainable. A favourite author with me at one time was Angela Brazil, all of whose stories were set against a boarding school background. But Angela Brazil had to be read on the sly, for Mother thought her books trashy and a waste of time.

I often wonder if children today use their imaginations or live in their own private fantasies as I did. Very often I would act out in my imagination the part of a book's hero or heroine. I have plotted against pirates along with Jim Hawkins and I have trembled with Jane Eyre as the first Mrs. Rochester rent her bridal veil in maddened

jealousy. I have been shipwrecked with Masterman Ready and on
Pitcairn Island with Fletcher Christian. I have been a medieval page
in Sir Nigel and Lorna Doone madly in love with 'girt Jan Ridd.' I
count myself most fortunate. There is much to be said for a
childhood deprived of some material advantages.

Chapter XXIV

One of our childhood institutions was the Saturday penny – as we
grew older and as even then, inflation cut into its value it was
upgraded first to a sixpence and then to a whole shilling. The penny
was almost always spent on 'sweets'. In a nation that surely must
rank highest as consumers of 'candy', what a wealth we had to
choose from in the little general stores. There was one of these small
shops opposite us, though to reach it we had to cross two main roads
separated by a triangular green on which was erected a monument to
the men of the Seventh Wilts who fell in the Great War. Later this
green was eliminated and the memorial moved in an effort to make
the intersection less dangerous for traffic. But when we were
children off to spend the Saturday penny, we were always warned to
look both ways before we sallied across. This particular little shop
changed hands rather frequently but we always seemed to make
friends with the proprietors and so our errands often took a long
time as a chat invariably followed the purchase unless there were
many customers.

A favourite purchase by small children, ourselves among them,
was packaged sherbet. This was not the sherbet of the icecream
family but a sweet effervescent powder done up in a brightly
coloured paper triangle. At the apex, a hollow stick of black licorice
protruded with which we dipped the powder into our mouths where
it fizzed and stung ever so slightly.

Sometimes our coins were spent on a pennyworth of sweets
chosen from a wide variety of confections of all shapes, sizes,
colours and flavours, displayed in huge glass jars – acid drops,
striped humbugs, glacier mints, toffees, chocolates, fruit bonbons,
buttered brazils or walnuts. Many of these sold for two ounces a

penny while others were more expensive. Often when Mother and I settled by the fire for a chat or a read, she would send me to the shop for a twopenny bar of chocolate (quite large in those days) and we would share it along with our confidences. She always left the choice to me and at various times we enjoyed Fry's Chocolate Cream, Cadbury's Dairy Milk Flake, Rowntree's Fruit and Nut bar. The choices were excruciating. In addition to our own Saturday purchases, Dad would usually buy a quarter or half pound of sweets for weekend consumption.

At Christmas we usually had some very beautiful boxes of chocolates given us. Often they were expressions of thanks from people for whom my handy father had done small kindnesses. Mother rationed the chocolates to us very carefully and we used the boxes to keep our treasures in – treasures such as paper dolls, beads, crayons, transfers and other impedimenta of childhood, trivia dear to the hearts of little girls everywhere.

During our childhood, chewing gum began to appear in the shops and became quite popular. But Mother forbade it and except for the odd occasion when we sneaked a stick we did not become gum chewers. I vetoed it in my classroom and still regard it as a loathsome habit.

Every Thursday, Father used to go to Devizes for the weekly sheep and cattle market. After depositing his auctioneer employer at the market he would walk around the old and interesting town. Devizes had a special place in Dad's heart. It was the town which served the villages he had lived in as a child and young man, and it was where he and Mother began their married life and where both May and I were born. He would meet old friends and some of Mother's relatives in town for the market, and drop in the town's beautiful old churches and browse in the very fine privately owned museum. When he came home, often very late at night, he invariably had some treats – perhaps a 'lard' cake from Strong's, a locally famous bakery, some special sweets and regularly for many years a copy of 'Tiger Tim' for May and 'The Rainbow' for me. These were comic papers for children – though not comics in the American genre. Serialized stories, old and new in pictorial, caption and narrative form were the main attractions, but the papers also contained crossword puzzles, tidbits of information, math puzzles, jokes and other trivia with general appeal for children. May and I read both avidly, arguing their relative merits and if Dad was late we would stay awake long after we had been sent to bed in order to get our papers. Dad would sometimes bring us back glue-backed sheets of such things as birds, butterflies or flowers. We could pull them apart and stick them into notebooks writing names underneath. As we grew a little older, to the comics was added every month an installment of Arthur Mee's *Children's Encyclopedia*. This very popular publication could be purchased in bound volumes or in magazine format. We collected them all and Mother always intended to have the magazines bound but somehow it was never done. The information was not arranged alphabetically but in categories – science, math, stories, poetry, history, geography, etc., and consisted of illustrated articles written in informative, easy to read prose, geared for children. I loved them and waited anxiously for each copy to come out. I know that my consistent reading of them added greatly to my store of general knowledge. Another fine publication was 'The Children's Newspaper' and I enjoyed seeing it but only occasionally for we never subscribed to it.

We also enjoyed the fruits of Father's visits to Bath whither he took his employer regularly to visit his aged father. Dad would always find something unusual and tasty from Bath's beautiful food shops – Bath buns, biscuits called Bath Olivers, a new sweetmeat called praline, a piquant spread called 'Gentleman's Relish', sometimes a Bath chap. The latter is made from the meat off a boiled pig's head, pressed into a cone covered with bread crumbs and eaten cold. This, though delicious, we ate with care for we hated the thought of gristle and I always wondered about the pig's eye. Mother occasionally bought a pig's head and boiled it herself. She and Dad ate it with relish, but the cold glassy stare of the eye, the hairy ears and nostrils repelled me. The Bath chap was infinitely preferable. Another taste treat that came from Bath was a red-skinned sausage eaten cold that I believe was called 'polony'. Our favourite gourmet item from Bath however was pork pie – a mound of tender pork in a coat of gelatine inside a pastry case.

Occasionally I went to Bath with Dad and Mr. Hooper and then Dad and I had several hours to explore the beautiful Georgian city, its ancient abbey, Pump Room and Assembly Rooms as well as the Roman Baths. I loved the sightseeing but the zenith of such trips was tea at the Red House – crumpets and cream cakes. Mr. Hooper nearly always gave me a half-crown and then some shopping had to be squeezed in before the thirty-two mile ride home.

Dad liked to give Mother little unexpected presents, most of which he purchased in Bath. He had an unerring eye for trinkets and semi-precious stones which were beautiful and unusual though of necessity, of little intrinsic value. She used to scold him for spending money but she was pleased really and always wore her brooches, pendants, and bracelets with much pride. A few I still wear today, though some I lost when our Glen Rock house was broken into some years ago.

As I grew older Dad's gifts to me whenever he went somewhere unusual began to take the form of books. The nucleus of my own personal library was formed by my school prizes, books awarded annually at a special ceremony in the Town Hall for outstanding achievement in school work. I received a prize every year – at first for rank in class, later for History, English, Latin and Divinity. Chosen from the classics, the prize books were beautifully bound, stamped with the school crest and suitably inscribed inside. I valued them highly – in fact I still do. In 1945 I sent them along with other books, in a box, ahead of me to the United States, where they made an impression on my father-in-law, who, himself a 1900 graduate of the University of North Carolina, had at one time taught Latin and Greek in Durham, North Carolina.

Chapter XXV

After Mother had budgeted carefully for rent, food and fuel the next big expense was clothing for the family. We were probably among the best dressed children of our day in the town. Mother believed in quality before quantity and liked plain serviceable clothes which looked attractive because they were good and because she had impeccable taste in colour and style. She sometimes dressed us exactly alike – we were occasionally taken for twins since May was not much taller than I – but more often Mother preferred to dress us coordinately with subtle differences in colour, material or style suited to our separate personalities.

When we were very young we were, of course, victims of the unrealistic dressing of children as miniature adults, but fortunately there was soon a move to freer, more appropriate clothing of which Mother was quick to take advantage. I remember the button boots we wore to school as infants. The buttons had to be fastened with a button hook, time consuming for Mother on dark winter mornings as the task was beyond our manual dexterity. The variable climate could be counted on to be damp and cold for several months of the year and so it dictated the type of clothing worn. Layers which could be easily added or removed were best protection against the weather's vagaries and wool was the fibre which predominated for nine months of the year with cotton in the summer and silk for best. The wool, we were told, most likely came from sheep in Australia or New Zealand and was woven in Yorkshire, while the cotton grew in Egypt or India and was made into material in Lancashire.

Our underwear was rather startling. We wore knitted vests all year round and combinations (which we hated) in winter. These were like skin tight jump suits with seat flaps and longish legs. These garments were made of wool and Mother always tried to afford a brand known as 'Chilprufe' which was soft and comfortable to wear and proof to some extent against the laundry shrinkage to which woollen garments are prone. No one in those days seemed to be allergic to wool – in fact, I had never heard the word 'allergy' until I got to America.

Over vest and combinations we wore something known as a 'Liberty bodice'. This was a sleeveless tightly fitting garment buttoned up the front and made of a stretchy cotton material which was supposed to give support to growing bodies. The bodice had innumerable buttons and loops and suspenders, to hold stockings up, could be attached. In summer our panties or 'knickers' as we called them, were of white cotton but in winter they were of heavy cotton knit, fleece lined, and navy blue in colour. Stockings were usually wool and black and in spite of the Liberty bodice's provision for suspenders, were held up by garters which Mother made out of elastic purchased by the yard. She was always careful to make them tight enough to hold our stockings up but not so tight that circulation would be constricted. It was a relief to get into summer's white cotton socks. Before we wore new underwear, Mother reinforced every button hole and added stitches to every button. She did the same for her own lingerie and my father's underwear and shirts. When a hole appeared in heel or toe of socks or stockings she darned it so beautifully that it was a work of art. I ran innumerable errands to Harraway's in the Parade to buy darning wool, cotton, elastic and ribbon. Since she washed on Monday and ironed on Tuesday, she always did the mending on Tuesday evenings.

Mother had a small Singer sewing machine which was turned by hand. Though she rarely made dresses for us, she used the machine for curtains and turning sheets sides to middle and for other repairs which would extend the life of household draperies and linens.

She was an expert knitter. We rarely saw her sitting by the fire of an evening without her knitting. She made my father's socks and made many 'jumpers' (sweaters) and cardigans for us. When we were very small she knitted dresses for us. Once we had matching cherry red dresses with lacy skirts – fine examples of the knitters' art. Once too, she made ribbed dresses of similar style but different colours. May's was navy blue with emerald green trim and mine was a light tan which Mother called 'biscuit' with mauve stripes. As we grew older she liked to dress us in pleated navy skirts with blouses and cardigans. Often she used wool that looked like tweed when it was knitted up. She also knitted gloves for us and, at one time, I remember we were the proud possessors of white fur hats and muffs.

Though she rarely purchased anything from them, she had catalogues sent to her from several London department stores. We looked forward to the arrival of these very much. We leafed through the booklets from Pontings', Barkers', Selfridges' and Marshall and Snelgrove, making up imaginary orders and, once Mother gave us permission to do so, cutting out the pictures of the models and pasting them into booklets. Once she ordered very expensive scarlet blazers with brass buttons from Selfridges' and when we wore them with navy blue pleated skirts and white blouses, we were the envy of all our friends. Mother's favourite store was the exclusive Marshall and Snelgrove. It was here that her employer, Mrs. Hume, had shopped. In early spring of 1944, Mother and I went on a shopping expedition – the last time I was to go to London with her. We went to Marshall and Snelgrove where, no longer economy minded, she bought my wedding dress. In keeping with war-time economy, it was not a white gown but a beautiful powder blue wool dress and jacket.

We always had best Sunday clothes as opposed to everyday ones. Best clothes were always purchased a little on the large side so that after a few months as Sunday clothes they could then be worn to school. Once when they were all the rage we had tussore or shantung silk dresses. They were in the beautiful natural colour of the lustrous fabric imported from the Orient.

When I was about ten, Mother felt it would be more economical to buy material by the yard and to have our clothes made. We used to go with her to Sloper's, a shop in Kingsbury Street, to choose the fabric and it was then taken to a couple of middle-aged ladies who lived near us in a small cottage. They did dressmaking for a living, supporting themselves and their widowed mother. After much deliberation, we would decide on a style and a week or so later the garments would be finished. For many years the Misses Hutchins dressed us well, stylishly and economically. Their tiny house fascinated me. Every available surface was covered with embroidery. There were cushion covers, footstools, pictures, tablecloths, runners, a firescreen and even the mantel over the fireplace had an embroidered pelmet. I could only conclude that not content with sewing for a living, they took up a different version of the needle art for relaxation.

The biggest items in the clothing budget were winter coats, raingear and shoes. Mother liked navy blue tailored coats and I usually was able to wear May's for a second winter, so she only had to purchase one at a time. Always we had good raincoats and rubber Wellington boots. Mother always bought shoes at Hurd's in the High Street. She liked the brands he sold better then those carried at Mundy's, the other shoe store in town. Owen Hurd was something of a character, a curmudgeonly man who was reputed to be quite rich. He was a chronic complainer with a particular down on teachers who, he used to say, worked only half a day, half a week and half a year. He fitted us for shoes for many years, brown and black sensible Oxfords for everyday, black patent slippers for best, Russian boots for winter and Wellingtons for rain, woolly bedroom slippers and rubber soled play shoes or 'daps' as we called them.

When I went to the Grammar School I had to wear a uniform. This consisted of a navy blue gym slip. Made of serge it had three box pleats front and back attached to a sleeveless square yoke and was worn over a white blouse and cinched in at the waist with a braid sash tied in a sailor knot. Our shoes and stockings were black and we wore the maroon school tie. We were also expected to have a school blazer – maroon with the school crest (a castle) and date (1550) on the breast pocket. If we wore a cardigan it had to be maroon. Our winter coats and raincoats were navy blue and we wore shapeless brimmed hats – black beaver in winter and panama straw in summer. The hatband was maroon with the school crest in front. In the summer we wore tan cotton dresses with the school tie. We were very proud of our uniform and there is much to be said in favour of school uniform. Mother saw that my clothes were of good quality. I still, of course, needed regular clothes for best and a white silk dress had to be purchased. This was worn at the annual Prize Giving ceremony held in the Town Hall at the end of every year. Around Christmas, each 'set' or house had its annual social, held in the school dining room and this required a party dress.

Chapter XXVI

We were always very excited when Mother made a rare purchase of clothing for herself. Any coat or dress that she would want to wear, for she liked good quality, only materialized after long and hard savings, squeezing an extra penny here and there. The 'best' store in town was called at that time 'Paris House' and, rather bending the truth, advertised fashions as being straight from the French capital. Once at sale time Mother bought a beautiful cocoa coloured coat with lustrous dark fur collar and cuffs. But it was in the style of the mid-twenties, knee length with a hip level front belt, and that spring hem lines drastically descended and waistlines drastically rose. Mother rarely wore her longed-for coat. I felt her anguish keenly and even now the memory of her frustration and disappointment pains my heart. Not only did she have no coat to wear but she had wasted, what to her was a lot of money.

When I was very young, Mother wore a very elegant coat of imitation astrakhan or Persian Lamb. When it was no longer wearable for her she had it made into a beautiful child's coat which was first worn by May and later by me.

Mother had been married in a navy blue suit which, she was fond of telling us, was made of the finest wool serge and elegantly cut with the long fitted coat fashionable at the end of the Edwardian period. But all that remained of her wedding finery was her hat, a beautiful wide creation of white tulle, the brim lined with pink and decorated with tiny pink roses, lilies of the valley and blue forget-me-nots. We used to play with it as children when we went to the top room and dressed up in clothes of bygone days stored in a yellow tin trunk.

Mother was tall and well built with the full figure so much admired at the time of her youth. When young, she had a mass of straight dark brown hair which was piled over a frame into a knot on top of her head. She went grey very early – pepper and salt in my earliest memory, gradually changing to a lovely silver. My father for

many years was adamantly against her cutting her hair. She wore it
in plaits coiled over her ears, but one day, saying nothing to anyone,
she had it cut off, permed and waved. She looked years younger and
everyone, including my father, liked it. Mother had a very beautiful
complexion, soft and completely blemish-free. Her nose, which had
been broken in a cycling accident when she rode at night into closed
iron gates, was not quite straight but this lent interest to her face.
Her teeth though white and even were not good and she was
wearing false teeth before she was forty. But this in no way marred
her looks. She had an air of serene contentment about her which was
perhaps the mainspring of her attraction. While working for Mrs.
Hume, an artist friend of hers had asked if he could paint my mother
saying she had the face of a Burne Jones angel. Mother declined,
largely, I think, because she thought his intentions might be less than
honourable. But I agree with that unknown artist when I look at one
particular photograph of my mother. It was taken on the occasion of
my sister's christening. Mother dressed in a skirt and white shirt-
waist is holding the six-week-old infant dressed in the beautiful robe
of the Sharpe family. Its white lace skirt cascades down over
Mother's dark one. Perhaps Mother looks more like a young
Madonna than a Burne Jones angel – but to whichever one compares
her at that moment – she was certainly beautiful.

Chapter XXVII

As an elementary school child and until I was eleven I went to the
Church of England school known as St. Mary's Girls'. This school
and the Infants' School were housed in the same building but
operated as separate schools each with its own staff and headmistress. The Infants' School had two teachers in addition to the head,
who taught a class as well as performing her administrative duties.
The Girls' School, like its counterpart St. Peter's Boys' School, had
four staff members working under a teaching principal. Only about
half the teachers were fully qualified, some being known as
uncertificated teachers. These had left a secondary school with a
good academic record – this was a prime requisite – and had become

pupil teachers, trained on the job by the head teacher. The English have always had a belief in learning by doing as evidenced in trade apprenticeships and the system of articling young men to certain professions such as some branches of law and surveying. In due course, pupil teachers became uncertificated teachers performing all normal duties for low pay and with no prospect of advancement. The majority became fine teachers largely because they felt a calling for teaching and considered it a vocation. The pupil teacher system disappeared from the English scene many years ago and uncertificated teachers were gradually phased out by death and retirement.

The trained teachers who held a teaching certificate granted by one of the leading universities, had attended a Teachers' Training College for two years. There were many such institutions dotted all over England. They were small and separate for men and women. There, young people who had done well in secondary school continued their general education, took some pedagogical courses and practiced teaching in certain schools under the guidance and supervision of their lecturers, the school head and the teacher of the class to which they were assigned. Teachers who held university degrees taught almost exclusively in the academic secondary schools at a considerably higher salary.

The student body of St. Mary's, following the common organizational pattern, was loosely divided into seven standards and a child would stay in each standard only as long as it met his educational needs. Children tended to be divided according to ability or accomplishment rather than age, and individual promotions and sometimes demotions took place whenever they were deemed appropriate. The 'best' teacher, in the judgment of the head, was always assigned Standard V, for this was the group that would face the 11 plus examination and here children were coached and prepared for entrance to academic secondary school. Bright children – scholarship material – sometimes spent as long as two years in Standard V, either waiting till they were old enough to take the exam or trying again if they had failed the first time. The headmistress taught Standards 6 and 7 – girls who had not passed the 11 plus and were staying on in St. Mary's till fourteen or fifteen to complete their education. A group of the most responsible girls became 'monitors' and assumed some small duties helping with the younger children. The emphasis in Standards 6 and 7 was on practical subjects and their education aimed to make girls self-sufficient and responsible.

The Marlborough town schools were really expanded versions of village schools and as such they succeeded, by and large, in educating

children according to their ability, meeting individual needs and
differences. Bright children were identified early, given every assist-
ance and encouragement, and pushed to the limit of their growing
capabilities. Slower children were able to go at their own pace, were
tutored and helped but expectations for them were never unreasonable and unrealistic. Bright children sometimes helped slower ones,
older children, younger ones. There was a family feeling in the
school which perhaps was a natural extension of life in the large
families that were common at that time and in that place.

The Girls' School building consisted of two large barn-like rooms
which were divided into classrooms by folding or portable screens.
Opening the screens made supervision of a large number of children
by a single teacher possible, thus giving the head some freedom for
her administrative duties and the opportunity to observe and help
her staff during school hours. It also did away with the need for
substitute teachers. When a teacher was absent classes simply dou-
bled up. One advantage was that classes could be put together for
subjects such as sewing and singing and the opened up rooms
accommodated the morning and evening assemblies which began
and ended the school day with prayers and hymns. In my modern
'egg-crate' type of school in New Jersey, I often wished for the
expandable classroom.

The rooms were drab in the extreme with high windows, poorly
lit and draughty for with true British love of fresh air windows were
open winter and summer alike. In winter, the rooms were heated by
black pot-bellied stoves which consumed coke, rationed to the
teacher and shovelled in by her. Each stove was surrounded by a
high black iron guard. Close to the stove one almost scorched but a
few feet away children shivered. The desks were antiquated – some
of them forms, seating four or six children, with iron feet screwed to
the floor. Their only merit was that they eliminated noise from
shuffling desks and chairs. Each seat had its inkwell, the ink mixed
from powder by the teacher or pupil and the wells filled on Monday
and washed on Friday. Cloakroom facilities were crowded and
inadequate, while toilets were across the playground. As town
children we were fortunate to have the flush variety. The asphalt
playground, surrounded by walls that effectively shut out any ray of
sunshine, was small and sloping. Here we lined up every morning,
played at morning and afternoon recess, and endured the daily
physical education drills which were considered very important for
our health and well-being. Only in the very coldest or wettest
weather were we kept in for recess or our exercises. My sister and I

were always well and warmly dressed in winter with good strong waterproof shoes, but it was no uncommon sight to see a child blue with cold, shivering on the playground.

Nevertheless our basic education was good in spite of our poor facilities and knowing nothing better we were happy, content and proud of our school. If St. Mary's taught me nothing else, it demonstrated that fine buildings do not necessarily make for a good education.

The small rural schools in England at that time, were made or marred by the head teacher who was a despot in school and a power to be reckoned with in the community. Most of these men and women were dedicated to providing for their pupils the best possible education and in order to do so, they gave unstintingly of time and effort. They had the advantage of knowing their students, their families and their backgrounds extremely well and so were able to meet the needs of individual children. They were responsible for the training of young teachers and the continued supervision of all their teachers. The competition that existed between school and school for academic and athletic achievement spurred their efforts. Also they, their schools, teachers and pupils, were exposed to the constant possibility of inspection – both from the Local Education Authority which in our case was the Wiltshire County Council, and from Whitehall – His Majesty's Inspectors commonly known as H.M.I.s. Approximately every three weeks each school was liable for a full scale inspection. Teams of inspectors would descend and remain in the school for days at a time. Every facet of school life – classroom performance, curriculum, teachers' plans, examination results – all would come under the critical eyes of the inspectors and woe betide the head teacher, staff member or student who did not measure up. If deemed necessary, plans for change would be implemented and a follow-up inspection would ascertain that they were being acted upon. In addition to the anticipated inspections, inspectors would drop in when least expected and both, as teacher and pupil, I experienced on several occasions the sinking feeling when the dread news of 'H.M.I.s in the building' came down the grapevine.

History and geography were perhaps my favourite subjects in St. Mary's. To a great extent they were part of the comprehensive language arts teaching which permeated our entire learning. We learned a good deal of both from stories and literature for, when appropriate, everything that we discussed was pinpointed in time and space. Every September we were given a good explanatory lesson on time with time lines and charts to illustrate it. My first history lessons in Marlborough about the Ancient Britons, Romans, Saxons, Danes and Normans were supplemented by walks to Norman churches, Roman roads, British graves with which our area abounded – we kept illustrated notebooks on local history and our textbooks were a joy to read and study. On the subject of British textbooks I can only say I consider them superb. At the elementary level our history texts emphasized daily life and especially children's life in the past. They were well-illustrated, often used original sources and were graphically written and eminently readable. On visits back to London from the States, I would always try to get to Foyle's Book Store where every conceivable British school text could be found and I could happily lose myself for a few hours.

Geography too started out on the local level but proceeded to the study of England – from thence to the British Empire. We were thoroughly indoctrinated with its fading glories. Even today when I visualise the map of the world it is the Mercator projection with the British Isles in the centre and red patches all over the world denoting the empire on which the sun never set, which comes into my mind's eye. Our study of the empire inspired a certain amount of patriotic fervour in us only dimly understood but it certainly was good for our geography.

We learned little science in St. Mary's except for nature study. Sometimes when the sun shone, we were told to put books and pens away and we would go for a nature walk studying the local flora and fauna. Often the nature walk would be the topic for our next week's composition. Again we kept notebooks recording our observations and illustrating them and we would take specimens back for further study in the classroom. Early in spring we would bring the big sticky buds of the horse chestnut into school, keep them in water and watch them unfold into the beautiful five and seven-fronded leaves. A jar of frog spawn always found its way in too and we would watch the black spot in the jelly-like eggs grow into tadpoles and finally into little frogs, when we would return them to the closest stream or pond. Broad beans used to be grown in a jar, held close to the side by a piece of wet blotting paper and we would watch first the root and then the shoot break out of the bean. Other favourite experiments were to grow mustard and cress on a piece of damp flannel and a hyacinth bulb in a jar of water. I liked the spontaneity of our nature, history and geography walks – again something I missed in the United States where permission slips from parents were required before any expedition outside the school could be taken.

In addition to academics we were taught sewing and knitting.

Two whole aftenoons a week were given up to these subjects. Three classes were put together and two teachers taught the intricacies of knitting and basic sewing while the third read aloud. I remember *Puck of Pook's Hill,* Kipling's story saga of British history and *Peter Pan* and being reprimanded for listening so intently that my knitting and sewing lay neglected. Though I am now a good knitter, I had some difficulty learning it in the beginning and neither was I very good at sewing. My 'run and fell' seam never seemed to give satisfaction and I had a habit of pricking my finger and leaving bloodstains on the pristine whiteness of my work. However since this was the only instruction I ever received in the needle arts I am grateful for it. I am by no means sure however, that such instruction belongs in the elementary school. I believe we were too young and that the eye and hand coordination of many children was not ready for such close work. It was the one area in elementary school where I experienced difficulty and my first taste of failure. Minor though it was, I did not like it.

I liked music lessons much more. Our school day began and ended with the lusty singing of hymns and patriotic songs – 'God Save the King' and Elgar's Pomp and Circumstance March – 'Land of Hope and Glory' which well nigh superseded God Save the King as our national anthem; also I liked the haunting melody of Kipling's Recessional. We had regular music lessons in which we learned to read music using the tonic sol-fa system and calling the time value of notes by their old names of breve, semibreve, minim, crochet, quaver, semiquaver and demisemiquaver, names unused and practically unheard of today. Tunes too, were divided into bars rather than measures. Several classes were put together for music and singing, with one teacher playing the piano and another conducting the singing. Piano playing was a very important attribute for a teacher and was a requirement for positions in many elementary schools. We worked very hard on certain songs, usually English folk songs, with a few classics too, for we used to attend country music festivals where our school would sing in competition with classes from many other Wiltshire schools.

After the war, a group of English composers working together, rediscovered the ancient dance tunes and folk songs of England, edited them, rearranged them and brought them into renewed popularity. Ralph Vaughan Williams, Percy Grainger and Cecil Sharpe were chief among them. The wireless was an important vehicle for transmitting them to the people at large but a network of folk festivals was also set up all over England involving all levels of the population in listening to or singing the songs of old England and in watching or performing the country dances of yore. In this way regional, country and local songs and dances were revived in the hope of perpetuation.

As an elementary school child I went three times with the St. Mary's Girls' School Choir to the festivals held twice at Devizes and once at Trowbridge, in which groups from most of the Wiltshire schools participated competitively for silver trophies which were held by the winning choir for a year.

Going to the festival was a rare treat and an event of great excitement and importance in our lives. We went by bus and took sandwiches with us supplementing them with local delicacies purchased in the shops, eating lunch at midday break in the choral proceedings. We were marshalled in and out of our seats which had been specially installed in the Town Hall at Trowbridge and the beautiful old Corn Exchange in Devizes market place. We were very quiet and orderly and well disciplined in our exits and entrances and general behaviour for in this way too, we were in competition with our sister schools.

It was thrilling to sing our hearts out in such a large assembly, to do our best in our school choir and to listen attentively to other groups. The proceedings always opened with the unison singing of 'God Save the King', sounding to me then so much more impressive than 'My Country 'Tis of Thee' does now. They ended with the massed voices singing 'Jerusalem', the mystical poem by William Blake beginning 'And did those feet in ancient times.' It is a referencee to the legend that Christ at one time visited England's West Country and we, as children of that part of England, felt it peculiarly appropriate to us with the second verse especially stirring us with half-formed idealistic hopes for our future and that of our great country:

> Bring me my bow of burning gold
> Bring me my arrows of desire
> Bring me my spear – O clouds unfold
> Bring me my chariot of fire
> I will not cease from mental flight
> Nor shall my sword sleep in my hand
> Til we have built Jerusalem
> In England's green and pleasant land.

Chapter XXVIII

Nineteen hundred and twenty-eight was the year in which I became eleven and thus it was the year when I faced the trauma of the 11 plus examination. The results of this examination determined the type of secondary education a child received. In 1928 in Marlborough for people of very restricted means the options were limited to two. A child either went to the local Grammar School if he placed high enough in the examination, or remained in his former school until he was old enough to leave at fourteen or fifteen. There were about a dozen free places in the Grammar School offered annually and these went to the brightest children of parents whose income, after a means test, was judged sufficiently low. All other children had to pay – at that time the fees, I believe, were three pounds ten shillings a term, of which there were three in the year, but money was not enough – pupils were admitted on scholastic merit and when the thirty or so vacancies were filled, there was no recourse for the others but to stay on in St. Peter's or St. Mary's unless parents could afford a private school of which there were two in the town, though with very small enrollments, or go to a boarding school which was very expensive and so precluded most children.

During World War II legislation was passed and implemented at the end of the war providing secondary education in separate buildings for all children over eleven. This gave rise to buildings known as the Secondary Modern Schools and at the same time, the enrollment in the Grammar School was increased and more academic courses were introduced into the Secondary Modern Schools. The system was, however, still selective and in the minds of parents, students and employers secondary modern education was second best. Eventually schools went comprehensive at the discretion of local education authorities and school boards and when the money for the new buildings required could be found.

But in my day and for many years afterwards, every child of eleven or twelve took the first part of the 11 plus examination, generally given in March. This was in the nature of an IQ test and effectively weeded out the slower children who were then not subjected to further ordeals. The second and major part of the test consisted of several written exercises, computation, problem solving and mental tests in arithmetic and dictation, written composition and language, vocabulary, and spelling tests in English. When the results of these were known, the most promising pupils were invited to the oral examination, in which the headmaster of the Grammar School interrogated the child on a wide variety of topics and assessed his potential in the light of long experience.

Each grammar or secondary school in rural areas served a district drawing pupils from villages surrounding the town where the school itself was located. Since only about thirty places were available annually at that time in our district, one can readily see that competition was very keen, not only between individual students but also between schools. It was a matter of great importance to the careers and reputations of teachers and headteachers to gain as many grammar school places each year as possible. Bright children were identified early, given special help, pushed and coached by their teachers and their parents for at least a year before the examination. Educators today, especially in America, raise their hands in horror at the thought of so much pressure on children, but it seemed that most of us took it in our stride, accepting the examination – and its results – as inevitable and rising to the challenge as best we could. For the most part the pressure fell on the ablest pupils.

It was thought that I would win a place with no difficulty since I had learned to read early, and wrote with fluency. For a year before I was due to take the examination, I was kept after school for coaching and received extra homework over which my mother watched like a hawk. My sister, who was never a good student, had failed to win a place the previous year, and this was a matter of great concern to my mother and father. There was not enough money for a private school and so she had perforce to continue at St. Mary's, where she remained until she was fifteen. And therein lay the heartache caused by this selective system. There were always a few good students who did not quite make it and there were many families that faced the same problem that ours did – that of having children in different schools – one academically oriented and to a certain extent elitist, the other, in spite of the best efforts of teachers, second best. I know that this matter of different schools became a bone of bitter contention between May and myself and after I went to the Grammar School, we were never really close again as we had been as small children.

One could argue too that eleven is awfully early to make a decision which could affect a child's whole life. However, exceptions were made and if a late-blooming boy or girl showed great promise at thirteen or fourteen, he could be admitted then if he satisfied the powers that be of his ability. Even so I am sure many children missed the boat. But it was the best that could be offered at that time when money was in very short supply and it certainly meant that those of us who were fortunate enough to be admitted to a Grammar School received an education in the company of children of similar ability.

In the spring of 1928 then I took the examination. For three days, we took test after test after test. It was nothing new, for we had practiced taking the tests of many previous years. I was not nervous but on the vocabulary test there appeared a word totally unfamiliar to me. That word was 'almanac.' When I went home to report to Mother at lunch time I confessed that I did not know the meaning of the word. She called me a silly child and took my ignorance very seriously. Had it caused me to fail the examination? 'Almanac' haunted me until the results came out and I found I had been selected to take the 'oral' examination – the last hurdle. Needless to say I have never forgotten 'almanac'.

I would like to make one comment on the examination. One test was a composition – a choice of several titles was offered and several other questions were of the essay type. In our writing we were expected to display as much general knowledge as we could. The examiners marked us on content, form, grammar, usage, spelling – and background knowledge in the correct context. They paid little attention to handwriting for we were working against time. How vastly different from the true/false, multiple choice testing in vogue today.

The oral examination which came several weeks later was really nothing but an interview. The headmaster of the Grammar School, Sidney Pontefract by name, was an elderly Yorkshireman with a florid complexion, walrus moustache, rimless glasses and an incipient paunch, very conservatively and correctly dressed in a grey suit. He cleverly drew me out to talk about the things I liked to do, and books I had read and asked me some questions about local history and geography. After about fifteen minutes my mother joined me and he talked to us both about the school and its long history and his hopes and aspirations for it in the twentieth century. Early in the summer the list of those who had gained admission to the school was released and I was among the pupils from St. Mary's

Girls' School who were successful. I had received an excellent grounding at St. Mary's and am grateful to Miss M.E.N. Pearce, the headmistress who took as her personal responsibility the special coaching of her scholarship girls.

Miss Pearce had a noteworthy career as an educator and after retirement distinguished herself still further by serving on the Town Council and becoming Mayor of the town – one of the few women mayors in England at the time. She ran the town as she had run her school – well and efficiently. Always something of a martinet, she was nevertheless kind and understanding and always had high but not unrealistic expectations for her pupils. She had in no small degree what so many older English teachers develop – a commanding presence. She could walk into any room and a hush would descend and all children would stand in respectful silence. When I returned to England long after I was married I would sometimes meet her in the High Street and stop for a chat. I had the feeling that I was a little girl again and she was still my teacher.

Marlborough Grammar School had been founded by Edward VI in 1550 in a building that had once been a medieval hospital. For many years it educated the fee paying sons of local merchants, farmers and craftsmen. The original building was no longer in existence and after the founding of Marlborough College, as a school for the sons of clergymen in 1843, the Grammar School went into something of a decline while the college grew into one of the most distinguished of England's famous public schools. When the Education Bill of 1870 was passed it mandated elementary education for all and secondary education for the able, and at that time, the Grammar School became the secondary school serving the Marlborough district. For the first time it educated girls as well as boys, those who could qualify academically and whose parents could pay the modest fees. A certain number of places were reserved for children in financial need. This need was determined by a sort of rudimentary means test which caused some resentment among the poor. Though the school in my day was no different from other secondary schools all over England, yet it was a source of pride to us that we bore the name 'Grammar School', marking the school's roots in antiquity. We wore as the school badge a representation of Marlborough Castle and the date 1550.

When Marlborough Grammar School went comprehensive several years ago, it ended a long career spanning over four centuries as a school catering to students identified as being of high ability. The occasion of the school's demise as such was marked by a banquet served in Tudor style and attended by many old pupils. Unfortunately I was not among them.

Some in the town mourned its passing feeling that a link with the past had been broken. My education at Marlborough Grammar School was good and I was proud to be a pupil there, but that type of education must today be classed as elitist. The movement towards comprehensive education is part of the movement towards fuller democracy with equal opportunity for all.

Chapter XXIX

Going to the Grammar School changed my life considerably. My entrance there seemed to draw a line of demarcation between the security of childhood and the uncertainty of early adolescence. Life was never the same again. The blind faith I had in my parents was now in my mind open to question. For the first time I realised how poor we were compared with most of my fellow students – none of whom were rich. I clearly understood that my way of life in school would necessarily be dictated by the fact that there was very little money – much less than average. My mother who always held the purse strings was an excellent manager. She saved a little consistently and had encouraged the saving habit in us. We ate well, were always well dressed but all Mother's careful planning and strict economy could not provide me with sports equipment, art supplies, books, holidays abroad and other scholastic extra-curricular opportunities that were available for a price. They were entirely out of our reach and both she and I recognised it. I know her heart bled for me, but to my credit I never complained for fear of hurting her. Scholastically I was up against much stiffer competition but after some initial difficulty with physics and geometry I forged ahead to the top or near the top of my class – a position I managed to maintain for the entire time I was a pupil there. I enjoyed and rose to the challenge of algebra, chemistry and biology, French and Latin but it soon became obvious that my best subjects were English and history.

When I entered the Grammar School I was small for my age and not well-coordinated physically. I was very nervous in any athletic activity. I hated gym lessons and the acid remarks of the gym teacher and dreaded Thursday afternoons which were given over to games for the lower school – hockey and netball in the winter and tennis, volleyball and rounders in the summer. I was very shy with my peers and was slow to make friends. I was socially inept and to make matters worse soon earned the reputation of a bookworm, a brain, commonly and derogatively known as a 'swat'. Except for the new academic fields that were opening up, the first years in the new school were lonely an unhappy. But I did not complain and my mother was always there with unspoken sympathy and understanding. My sister and I grew further apart and we went through a period of constant quarrelling and bickering. Mother was very distressed and found this difficult to deal with. Soon the quarrelling stopped and we went our separate ways. May grew into a pretty vivacious girl very attractive to boys – in fact, for a while, she became quite boy crazy – another worry for my mother. It was however many years, before boys seemed to be aware of me or I of them.

Chapter XXX

My years at the Grammar School became happier as I went on. I became reconciled to my lack of athletic skill and took pleasure in the academics. I made a few very good friends, but was not very active in the social life of the school. This did not seem to worry me. I sang in the school chorus and enjoyed singing in the cantatas we presented annually. I remember musical settings of Tennyson's 'The Revenge', Browning's 'The Pied Piper of Hamelin' and 'The Jackdaw of Rheims' from the Ingoldsby Legends. I accepted the limitations that our poverty imposed with equanimity but did not assert myself to compensate for them.

I remember many of the teachers with pleasure and gratitude, recognising them for what they were – people over-gifted and over-qualified and underpaid for the jobs they were doing.

Science was taught by an extremely gifted man named A.A. Golding, also a fine cellist and leader of the school orchestra. He was universally loved and respected – a short, bald man with a beneficient expression behind thick lensed glasses. His favourite philo-sophical dissertation was based on the fallacy that lies behind the dictum – 'Eat, drink and be merry for tomorrow we die.' Few of us, he would say, will die tomorrow. He was the father of two sons, both brilliant students and athletes. One has become famous as the novelist and writer, William Golding, 1983 winner of the Nobel Prize for Literature.

"Bill" Golding was in the 6th Form when I entered the school in the fall of 1928. He was a stockily built boy of medium height with strongly marked features. In addition to being a very fine student he was an outstanding athlete. I remember my first summer in school watching the finish of a gruelling cross country race in which he battled for first place with a boy named Peter Marchant. Oddly enough I cannot recall which of them actually won but I do remember seeing both of them, sweaty and mudstained collapsing in sheer exhaustion. At the school Sports Day that same year Bill made a spectacular long jump which broke some existing records though I do not know the exact details. I shared in the pride felt by the whole school, and indeed the whole town when he won a scholarship to Oxford University.

A man named William Clayton (known irreverently as 'Old Bill' behind his back) taught us geography. He was a Cambridge man, holder of a rowing blue, but his brilliant promise had been blighted by the war. Severely wounded, he was deaf as a result. Loud voiced, he terrified us all. His lessons were delivered in short, sharp, staccato style phrases as he strode back and forth across the classroom like a caged lion. We took endless notes and made innumerable maps and charts. His methods never varied. He rarely marked our work and we never dared complain but we were scared not to do it. In the end we learned our way around the world as few children learn it today. This same master taught Latin. He railroaded it through in a similar fashion. It remained Double-Dutch for a long while but eventually we saw the light and suddenly found that we knew a great deal of Latin.

Latin began in the Third Form (age thirteen). Latin was taught to all the boys, but only a few selected girls were offered a choice between Latin and Domestic Science (Home Economics). When I was given the option I discussed it with my mother. She decided I should take Latin, saying that all I needed to be a good cook was a shilling cookery book and a 'haporth' (Half-pennyworth) of com-mon sense. I have turned out to be a reasonably good cook doing it I might add on 'the haporth of common sense' as I generally dispense with a cookbook. I never regretted my (her) decision to take Latin, though it ceertainly exercised me at times. It stretched my mind more than any other subject, though stretching the mind is what education is all about. Learning Latin gives one a marvellous insight into a civilisation that ruled and moulded the world. It brings English down to the bare bones and gives one a basic understanding of one's own tongue. I learned Latin concurrently with French and that is the way it should be studied, hand in hand with a Romance language. We covered a lot of ground with our demanding and singularly unhelpful teacher. He taught us through fear and with speed – we were afraid not to keep up. Grammar, declensions, conjugations, gerunds and gerundives led us to Caesar, Virgil, Horace and Ovid. Later when a new young teacher came we went on to Cicero, Livy and Tacitus. This young man was to write on one of my last report cards 'an excellent Latin student, but is under the erroneous impression that she is better than she really is.' I credit Mr. Clayton with inspiring the self-confidence that generated the remark, for in general, it was self-confidence I so sadly lacked.

Some of my Latin stayed with me. My son struggled with it in Glen Rock High School and I took him word by word through one of the books of the Aeneid. I could not help but contrast his brief foray into the world of Latin literature with all that we had covered at the same age. I also did a little tutoring in Latin, but now my Latin is naught but a pleasant though still stimulating memory.

For the first four years at school there were few changes in teachers. The staff remained virtually the same, year in, year out. Any new teacher was cause for rare excitement. But in 1932, the school numbers rose rather drastically, requiring staff augmentation and several of the older teachers reached retirement age and were replaced with younger people. Most important of all, a new headmaster was appointed to take the place of the retiring Mr. Pontefract. Poor Mr. Pontefract did not live long to enjoy retirement, for he succumbed shortly afterwards to appendicitis. He was the epitome of the conservative Englishman who for all his limitations had done a fine job for many years, as headmaster and, along with his wife, as a local leader in the Boy Scout movement. He is remembered kindly by the many Marlborough men and women educated under his tutelage.

His successor, A.R. Stedman, was a vastly different man – very talented, very dynamic. Under his leadership, the school grew in numbers and in the acquisition of scholastic and athletic honours. He expanded the staff, choosing young and gifted teachers.

I was entering the Fifth form when he came. It was at the end of this year that we took a very important examination – the Oxford School Certificate, a comprehensive examination regionally given, attesting to a successful completion of a secondary course in general education. Only those destined for college or university would continue on for two more years in the Sixth form. The others would leave school and become part of the labour force. It was thus a most opportune time for me that Mr. Stedman came. He himself taught English literature to the Fifth form. His approach to Charles Lamb, de Quincy, Coleridge, Wordsworth, Tennyson and Browning was electrifying in its stimulation. In addition, being somewhat given to digression during those periods, he opened windows into many areas of thought.

At the end of the year I passed the Oxford School Certificate examination. Two years later I took the Oxford Higher School Certificate in English, history French and Latin. After some discussion with my parents and Mr. Stedman it was decided that I should stay in the Sixth form a third year during which time I should read extensively and enter a university at the end of the year. The Wiltshire County Council gave me a very small financial grant for that year. A few months later Mother and Father decided that even with maximum monetary help, there was no way in which they could support me for four years in a university and half in chagrin and half in relief, I began to apply to two-year Teacher Training colleges. I applied to Whitelands College in London, Homerton in Cambridge and Salisbury in Wiltshire, and after acceptance at all three, I chose to go to Whitelands, one of the oldest and most prestigious of such institutions. I had to go to London for an interview with the Principal, Miss Dorothy Counsell. I was very nervous and she appeared large and very terrifying. She criticised my Wiltshire accent but my scholastic record was good and some weeks later, I received notification of my acceptance and so made plans to enter in September of 1936.

Teaching was not the career I wanted or one to which I felt particularly suited. But teaching and nursing seemed the only jobs open for girls who wanted to continue their education beyond secondary school but could not either for lack of ability and/or money gain a university degree. So many girls settled for teaching and counted themselves fortunate to have advanced even such a small bit up the ladder of life.

I wondered at the time, whether my third year in the Sixth Form was necessary or worthwhile – for I could have entered college a year earlier and so got out into the labour force and eased the financial burden on my parents. In retrospect it was a wonderful experience.

With no examination pressure – I read – books of all kinds in a kind of balanced diet prescribed by Mr. Stedman. I also continued studying French and Latin, both in rather desultory fashion. Mr. Stedman was a great proponent of religious education. Taught compulsorily, the rule was honoured in some secondary schools more in the breach than in the observance. Not so in Marlborough Grammar School, where it was taught as a branch of the history discipline. Mr. Stedman was in the process of writing two textbooks on religion at that time, both of which were to be widely adopted. I read the proofs and became madly enthusiastic about the history of the Hebrews and the early Christians. At that time, I was given to the worship of historical idols – Napoleon was one and St. Paul another – and I read avidly and voraciously anything I could find about my heroes. I shared my enthusiasm with my mother and she, dear, good, patient woman, must have been fed to the teeth with hearing about men long dead and gone.

Whitelands College was a Church of England institution and as such required a passing grade in a written test in religious knowledge known as the Archbishop's Examination. It was set by the Church and had to be taken by all who planned to enter a Church of England sponsored Teacher Training College. In preparation for this examination I studied for several months under the Rector of Marlborough at that time, a man named John Jones. He was tall, thin and angular – a man with a Christian's heart though overlaid with a veneer of middle class and intellectual snobbery.

Mr. Jones had prepared me for confirmation several years previously. At that time, a small group of young people met briefly and studied catechism and church doctrine with him in a rather perfunctory fashion, for a few weeks before the service in which the Bishop of Salisbury laid his hands on our heads and so made us full communicant members of the Church of England. Mr. Jones, assuming we had studied dogma and doctrine in schools, spent rather more time in examining our personal faith and commitment.

For my exam preparation, I used to meet Mr. Jones in his study in the cold, dark drafty rectory in the High Street near St. Peter's Church. We had some interesting discussions, and he made his library available to me. He was horrified, however, when I dared to question the divinity of Christ. He told me in no uncertain terms that there were some tenets of the faith that should be accepted absolutely and without question. I was caught squarely in the middle between Mr. Jones' conservative beliefs and the liberalism of Mr. Stedman's.

The examination papers were sent to Mr. Jones and one blustery Saturday morning in March, I answered questions for three hours in his study, with the rector acting as invigilator. Several other candidates whom I never met before or since took the exam along with me.

When the results came out, both Mr. Jones and Mr. Stedman were thrilled. I had passed with the highest honours and placed third in all England and first for Whitelands College. I received ten pounds worth of books from the Society for the Propagation of Christian Knowledge and later at college received a small gold cross engraved with my name, the date (1936) and Bishop of London's cross. It was presented to me at a college ceremony in person by the Bishop of London, a small lively man with grey hair and a pixie expression. In his gaiters and apron he bestowed it on me along with an episcopal kiss. I have the cross still and it is a cherished though rarely worn momento.

While at College I studied Divinity at the advanced level under a middle-aged Scotswoman named Elspeth MacKenzie. I have retained a good deal of the knowledge thus assimilated and still have a strong interest in the matter though as a teaching subject in the United States, my knowledge was never utilized. Since living in Chapel Hill I have led the study for women's groups or circles at the University Presbyterian Church. I enjoy doing this and find people most receptive and interested.

In keeping with his interest in religion, Mr. Stedman was also something of a hymnologist.

As in elementary school, so in the Grammar School, we always began and ended each school day with hymn singing and prayers. The whole school stood in class rows, packed like sardines into a small hall while we sang, prayed and listened to a short sermon and school announcements from the headmaster who stood in full academic regalia on a low dais. In the morning the hymn was usually a rousing martial tune or a lilting song of praise, in the evening the melody was likely to be sadder and more haunting. We belted out 'Onward Christian Soldiers' and 'Stand up, stand up for Jesus' with little regard for musicality, though our teachers did their best to introduce a few dynamics and elementary rules of diction. At the end of every term we sang, with lumps in our throats 'Lord Dismiss us with Thy Blessing' to a minor tune that I have never heard here. I have sung in a choir for many years in this country and sometimes a tune or anthem unfamiliar to everyone else will strike a chord in my memory and transport me back to the churches and schools of my childhood. Sometimes the words have been subtly altered and I must read along with everyone else for otherwise embarrassment might result.

Mr. Stedman introduced us to hymns and sacred songs outside the Hymns Ancient and Modern in everyday use. I remember 'Morning has broken' (in the last few years made into a popular song and still lovely), 'Glad that I live am I' and St. Patrick's Breastplate to name a few. Always he threw out the odd tidbit of history or background information which made him such a great teacher. In many ways he was much like my father in his endless search for knowledge for himself and with the gift of being able to transmit it to the young.

Two of the choir directors with whom we were associated at the West Side Presbyterian Church in Ridgewood, New Jersey, were distinguished hymnologists – George Litch Knight and John R. Rodland. They contributed much fascinating information about hymns, anthems and composers and I am most grateful to both for expanding my knowledge and linking it with information acquired many years ago in school in Marlborough. Today in Chapel Hill Dr. R. David Hoffelt, minister of the University Presbyterian Church is another fine church musician and hymnologist.

Chapter XXXI

All through childhood Mother and Father were quick to take advantage of any cultural opportunity that arose to round out our knowledge and give us additional experiences.

Marlborough had then and, I believe still does, a small though flourishing amateur operatic and dramatic society which worked hard to produce a play and musical presentation each year. The plays, with the exception of *The Importance of Being Ernest* and *The School for Scandal*, I seem to have forgotten, though the former drove Mother to reminisce about Oscar Wilde, his life, times and famous trial. His crime was never satisfactorily explained and it was years before I knew of what he was found guilty and for what he was imprisoned. The musicals made much more impression on me. Sitting on a hard chair in the Town Hall craning my neck to see the stage, I was on every occasion transported and enchanted. We saw many of the Gilbert and Sullivan operettas and in later years the Doyly Carte made no greater impression on me than the Marlborough amateurs. Perhaps my favourite though was Edward German's *Merrie England*. During the war, with David on leave from France, I saw a London production of it and found it just as tuneful and colourful, perhaps enhanced by the drabness of the times and the joy of being briefly together.

Occasionally a choral group from a larger town or city would visit Marlborough. Mother once left us in Father's charge while she went to the Town Hall to hear Handel's *Messiah*. She talked about it for days, telling us how the audience always stood for the Hallelujah Chorus and went about her work humming refrains from it. At the time I had only the haziest idea of what it was all about and it was not until I was in college that I heard it performed in its entirety. Since those days I have sung its choruses many times and often think of my introduction to it.

Other than Marlborough's amateur productions our theatre going was limited to a Christmas time visit to Bath, Swindon, Bristol, Reading or Southampton to see the pantomime. Typically British, a pantomime was a musical comedy revue loosely woven around a folk or fairy tale. Every pantomime had its Prince Charming (always played by a young girl) and its wicked witch (fat, blowsy and always played by a middle-aged comedian). Acrobats, jugglers, topical songs, comedy and dance routines were woven into the story which was presented in beautiful sets, costumes and lights with a joie de vivre that had a special charm for children. We would choose the pantomimes that seemed to appeal most from those presented in the surrounding towns and it was a gala occasion when we all set forth in December or January for the matinee, afterwards having tea in a restaurant before returning home. At various times we saw 'Aladdin', 'Jack and the Beanstalk', 'Hansel and Gretel' among others.

Field trips at school other than the spontaneous walks we would take, were unknown in the elementary school largely because of expense. In the Grammar School some were offered in the upper school at the discretion of the staff involved and had to be financed by the individual. I went with my French class to Bristol to see Moliere's *Le Bourgeois Gentilhomme* and to London to see *1066 and All That*, a revue and marvellous spoof on British history which I enjoyed immensely. I can still see Julius Caesar stiff-legged and cross-eyed stumping around among his legions as they gained their toehold in Britain in 55 B.C. and Henry VIII playing musical chairs with his six wives and Catherine Parr gaining the last remaining chair by unfairly sticking her knitting needles into the King's ample rear.

Once we went to a circus presented in a huge tent set up on the Common. We were enchanted but our pleasure was a little blunted by Mother's fear that fire would break out.

When I was a teenager in my latter years at the Grammar School a small and rather seedy repertory company visited Marlborough and stayed for several weeks, presenting an interesting series of plays. Shakespeare, Marlowe and Sheridan fitted in well with literature studies and the more modern ones, Shaw included, were thought-provoking as well as entertaining. Mother was delighted at the opportunity, but a little worried that the unorthodox life-styles of some of the players might influence us adversely.

But it was college that really introduced me to the London theatre. Matinee tickets were available for students either free or at minimal cost and for two years almost every Saturday afternoon would find us high 'in the Gods' at the Old Vic or Covent Garden soaking up the culture we had been lacking. College also gave me a taste of amateur theatricals but I was too shy and inhibited to experience any kind of pleasure or success and I confined my participation to singing in chorus and chapel choir.

Once again, I must emphasize the great debt we owed to radio for expanding literary and musical horizons. I am grateful to the high standard of B.B.C. programming and to my mother who read the *Radio Times* carefully and insisted that we listen to the music drama and commentaries that she felt were suitable and worthwhile.

Chapter XXXII

Living in a small town, as we did, my father soon became rather well-known, first as a craftsman, then as a man with a flair for accumulating and remembering knowledge and an ability to trans-mit it in a vivid raconteur's style. The town we lived in, Marlbor-ough, was the site of one of England's famous public schools – Marlborough College – and though, at that time, the division between town and gown was very marked several of the college masters and some of the boys' parents came to know my father through his beautiful woodwork. Some of them would stay in his workshop for long periods engaging, presumably, in intellectual discussions. Soon they were invited into our 'front' room, rarely used except at Christmas and for Sunday visitors, where my father's lovely furniture, carved, turned and inlaid was on display. All had a patina that came from beeswax – I can smell it still – and my mother's hand-rubbing and was a cause of surprised admiration from all who saw it. One of his visitors, I remember, was a Mrs. Wedgwood, a member of the famous china family. She was an elderly lady with delicate, finely chiseled features. Her son, an old Marlburian, had been killed in the war and she had erected a monument to him on the edge of the college playing fields.

My father, as I have already mentioned, drove a car for a local auctioneer. Some days he was away from home twelve to fourteen hours or even longer but other times he had no responsibilities and then he would spend hours in his workshop making his furniture and filling any orders for small items that came his way. The car he drove was kept in a garage in an alley off the High Street known as the Angel Yard, named after a temperance hotel that had once stood in the High Street. There was ample room for his workshop. It is said that Shakespeare had once acted in a troupe of travelling players in this yard and my father liked to tell that story very much. In telling it he gave it the ring of truth and authenticity. He was permitted to have the car for limited private use and we enjoyed many family outings, first in the blue Hudson touring car and later in a Talbot sedan. His work took him around the highways and byways of Wiltshire and he got to know the owners of many of the local timberyards, some of whom remembered his grandfather. He always had an eye out for English walnut, that very finely grained, darkly marked wood much in demand for fine furniture and now almost a wood of the past. He would often make his trinkets out of wood with some historical interest thus adding to their saleability. He bought some oak beams from St. Mary's Church when the belfry was restored and he also acquired some slightly charred beams from the Wolfhall tithe barn near Burbage, when it burned down. Since Wolfhall estate belonged to the Seymour family of whom Jane, the third wife of Henry VIII and mother of Edward VI, was the most famous member, it was interesting to speculate that she and her royal bridegroom had danced under those very beams at their wedding festivities in 1540.

My father and I used to write up little anecdotes such as this and where possible affix them to the bottom of bowls and other articles. To some extent we let our imaginations run on. My mother would irreverently say that if my father did not know something for sure, he made it up and today my husband accuses me of a like propensity.

Some of my father's friends persuaded him to exhibit his work at local craft shows and also in London and he was the proud winner of five gold medals. One was from a woodworking magazine and I think that was the one of which he was most proud. There was nothing that he could not do with wood – turning, carving, marquetry, fretwork. He turned out object after object of great use and beauty. For years he had nothing but a foot powered lathe and a little hand fret saw. As a child I wondered why his cheeks were always puffed out when he used this small saw until one day I realized it was to blow away the sawdust. For years he dreamed of owning a power saw and a 'Stanley' tool and eventually just before the Second World War his dreams were realized. He came to know A.E. Rowley of Bath, one of the most famous English marquetry experts of all time – in fact I still have in my possession one of Rowley's books with illustrations of some of his finest inlaid panels. My father also worked with a team of woodcarvers doing restoration work in Winchester Cathedral. He taught me the names of all the woods he used, most of them English but some from far away tropical places. Holly, I remember, as the whitest of wood used for snow in his marquetry pictures, while tropical ebony was the blackest. Yew, orange, when he first worked, darkened in a few years to port wine colour. That, of course, was the wood of the English longbow of medieval times and so highly valued that the tree was planted in churchyards to be safe from thieves in search of firewood. Dad's favourite wood was English walnut followed closely by English oak. He made my mother many lovely things – an oak lap desk inlaid with her initials, H.S., was his first present to her and a handkerchief box inlaid with a cube pattern and lined with cedar was another early gift. These are mine today and I also have the inlaid jewel box he made for my twelfth birthday and a little oak stool he made for me when I was about three. I have a few larger pieces of furniture but they do not hold quite the sentimental value of the aforementioned articles.

Father's woodworking brought him in contact with many people from different walks of life and we had a fairly regular string of visitors who came to buy woodwork but stayed to discuss religion, evolution, politics, books or any topic of the moment. These discussions would take place in our small living room – in winter the only heated room in the house – and my sister and I could listen in as long as we were seen and not heard. I well remember the local bank manager, rector, schoolmaster and Father talking and arguing and occasionally becoming quite heated in their wide ranging exchanges. Looking back, I realize what a privilege it was to be present at such meetings. Around 9 o'clock we would be sent off to bed and sometimes my mother would go to her room and leave the men to burn the midnight oil. I would hear the drone of their voices far into the night.

Dad was something of an authority on local history and he would often talk to church or charitable organisations on various aspects of it. He was much in demand as a speaker for he had the ability to capture and hold the interest of his audience. He never used notes, always speaking off the cuff and never hesitating for a word, fact or date. He also had a fund of Wiltshire tales, some of then rather racy, with which he would regale an audience in the broadest Wiltshire accent. He was also a rather keen member of Toc H, a semi-religious and mystical organisation of servicemen and ex-servicemen, formed in the trenches during World War I

Another interest cane into his life when I was about ten – that of beekeeping. I do not know who introduced him to apiarism but I do know that for several years it was an overriding passion with him. One of the largest and most prominent beekeepers in England at that time was a man named A.W. Gale, a Marlborough native. But my father did not agree with his methods and instead became the disciple of another well-known beekeeper named Larry Pearson. This latter was a most interesting man. His father was a clergyman and had at one time been chaplain to Queen Victoria. He was the youngest of a family of ten and as a bachelor lived with an unmarried sister who was the oldest of the family. Tall, thin and distinguished looking with a well-bred aristocratic voice, he struck up a friendship with my father though I do not know the exact circumstances of their first meeting. He and his sister lived in a small stone house with a lovely little walled garden in the tiny village of Vernham Dean on the borders of Wiltshire and Hampshire. The houses, theirs among them, clustered round the village green and pond where ducks and swans swam as in a rustic idyll.

By this time, my father, tired of being dependent on his employer's car had invested in a motorbicycle and sidecar. With Mother and myself tucked in the sidecar and with May perched pillion behind Dad, we made many Sunday afternoon trips to

Vernham Dean. This made my mother rather unhappy. She was not interested in bees and felt patronised by the Pearsons and would have much preferred to visit her sisters and brothers most of whom lived in villages near Devizes.

May felt as my mother did but I liked the Pearsons. They had many fascinating possessions and objects d'art. Chief among these, in my opinion, was a doll that had been given to the Pearson children by Queen Victoria. I looked at its seamed cracked face and stiff black hair with great awe, admiring its lace trimmed clothes complete with pantaloons, yellowed with age. Miss Pearson always had a little toy for us – one was a round glass-covered container in which we had to get a tiny mouse into what seemed an even tinier hole by our manual taps and tips and other manœuvres. There was a variety of old-fashioned children's books for us to browse through and lemonade made rather bitter by the addition of the peel and tiny cakes were always served to us. Sometimes another Pearson brother was there – a cassock-robed member of an ecclesiastical order. This man with his hawk nose and air of asceticism rather frightened us, yet he was unfailingly kind and polite, trying hard to bridge the gap between his own austere life and our childish interests. The Pearsons opened up a whole new world for me. There was talk of books, music and foreign places, for other members of the family were abroad. But always the talk came back to bees and more bees, honey and increased honey production.

Over the years we gradually lost touch with the Pearsons largely owing to my mother's lack of enthusiasm. Father and I missed them very much but both of us felt richer for having known them.

Father rented some ground about one-quarter mile from home and at one time kept some twenty hives. He also became one of the Wiltshire County bee experts going around to the villages near Marlborough for talks and demonstrations for which he was paid a modest fee. He was always very calm and quiet with his bees and rarely used either a veil or a smoker. He firmly believed that bee-stings (in moderation) would cure or alleviate 'rheumatism', that bane of middle age in the cool dampness of the English climate and I believe there was some medical support at that time for his theory. Only once did his bees turn on him and then he was badly stung and had to stay in bed for several days with swollen legs. Even then he took the blame saying he should never have gone near them in thundery weather. My mother's sympathy was in very short supply.

She dreaded, as indeed we all did, honey extracting time which came in the late summer. He had bought secondhand and very cheaply an extractor – a large metal cylinder with slots for two frames full of honey. These were then turned by hand and the honey was thrown out by centrifugal force into the bottom of the drum. Before the frames were inserted the wax toppings had to be cut off and the residue left after the turning had to be strained off through cheesecloth and put into sterilised jars and sealed. Our back kitchen, or scullery as we called it, was stripped of everything. We wore overalls and covered our hair but with all our precautions everything and everybody was sprayed with a fine sticky coating of honey. All this had to be done in the hot sultry weather of summer's end when wasps, flies and bees (our own and others) were a constant menace, screens, of course, being unheard of. Extraction was a process that could not be hurried and I think Mother, May and myself always prayed for a poor honey harvest. But Father was tremendously thrilled with the jars of clear golden honey. He would hold them up to the light and wax enthusiastic about clover honey, lime honey and heather honey. Each he felt had its own distinctive colour and flavour but I could never see how the bees could distinguish and felt sure our honey came from a mixture of many flowers. The sealed jars were stored in our third floor. We always hoped the honey would stay a clear golden liquid but most of it would begin to crystallise in a few weeks. Usually it went sugary and crunched when eaten but I remember one batch that stayed smooth when it solidified. We called it 'lardy' honey and liked it very much. We had honey for breakfast and honey for tea, Mother used it in cooking and often we sold it for one shilling and threepence per pound. I am sure we benefited nutritionally but I had too much of a good thing and I never touch honey now. We all, even my Father, who could not bear my mother's disapproval, used to heave a sigh of relief when the chore of honey extraction was over for another year.

Gradually he decreased the number of his hives, but up until the time of my mother's death in 1946, he kept one hive but had the honey extracted by a fellow beekeeper. When honey is taken from the hive it has to be replaced by sugar to feed the bees during the winter. Making the sugar into either syrup or hard candy was an added chore which my mother had to assume. During the war sugar was rationed but a special allotment was given to beekeepers in return for the production of honey, a valuable food in war-starved England.

Chapter XXXIII

The town's medical needs were met by two groups of doctors. When I was a child, Dr. Walter Maurice (pronounceed Morris) and Dr. Taylor practiced in a surgery on the lower side of the High Street near Dr. Maurice's home, which was a beautiful residence with gardens running down to the River Kennet. On the other side of the street Doctors Hayden and Wheeler practiced. Outside their surgeries each doctor put up his highly polished brass plate engraved with his name and degree, M.B. for medical doctor followed by Ch.B. if he was in addition a surgeon. The Maurice family had provided doctors for Marlborough for generations and they are still doing so, as the grandson of the Dr. Maurice I remember is in practice in the town today. The Maurices, though not titled, were important people in the vicinity, owning a great deal of land around a village called Manton hard by the town. Landowners, farmers, clergymen, teachers, lawyers and doctors they were very public spirited people serving the town in civic capacities, active in church work, leaders in organisations such as the Boy Scouts and in politics.

The Dr. Maurice of my childhood was a very tall round-shouldered man, bald with a fringe of grey hair at the back, a pronounced Oxford accent and an autocratic though rather vague manner that held little appeal for a small shy girl. He used to ride a bicycle to call on his patients with his bag strapped on behind. Surgery hours were held twice a day. To see the doctor in the surgery usually entailed a long wait. When we were ill, Mother would send Father to the surgery with a note and the doctor would call at the house later in the morning. She did not like to take us to the surgery, believing we would pick up additional germs from the waiting patients and she gladly paid the extra fee for a house call.

Mother thought Dr. Maurice was a very fine doctor and she always preferred to have him attend us, but as he and Dr. Taylor worked in rotation, it was anyone's guess which one would come. A doctor's visit was something of an occasion and by the time he arrived Mother had one or both of us, rosy with cleanliness, if not with fever, installed in her bed with the best counterpane spread over us. I was always glad if Dr. Taylor came for he would play with us and crack some jokes but I think I really liked him better because he always put his thermometer in my mouth whereas Dr. Maurice took my temperature rectally, which I thought indelicate and embarrassing. Dr. Taylor's wife died when she was quite young, leaving him with three small children and this caused me to lose faith in him. I could not understand how a doctor could let his wife die. I decided they must have been unhappy together, because I was quite certain that if my father was a doctor he would never let Mother die.

Another thing I always did when I was small was to take a good look in the doctor's bag when he opened it. Once, Mother announcing a new baby in the neighbourhood, had told us the doctor had brought it in his black bag. I was quite relieved each time I saw the bag contained no baby, for I did not want any interloper usurping my privileged position as the youngest member of the family.

Once the doctor had made his examination and identified the ailment, he then wrote out a prescription in what I thought was appallingly bad writing and this could be made up either in his own dispensary or the chemist's shop in the High Street. In serious cases the doctor himself would deliver the prescription to his dispensary and an errand boy would get it post haste to the patient.

The chemist's shop we used was Gantletts'. It was a small dark place and contained a shiny hall chair that I liked to sit on while admiring the huge bottles of coloured liquid which have been the sign of an alchemist's shop ever since the Middle Ages. One man who worked there was a tall gangling hunchback. I was frightened of him as he loomed out of the dim recesses behind the counter, in spite of his unfailing politeness and kindness. I much preferred the other chemist, a handsome man with a genial manner. The bottle of medicine was wrapped neatly in shiny white parchment and sealed at each end with bright red sealing wax. When you walked out with such a package everyone who saw it knew there was illness in your house.

In spite of prompt medical attention and correct dosage of the prescribed medicine most childhood illnesses meant several days in bed and a long period of recuperation. I remember the feeling of weakness on first getting up after several days in bed. There were no wonder drugs then for sulfa and penicillin did not appear until World War II.

Serious illnesses were taken care of in Savernake Hospital. This was a cottage hospital about two miles east of town just off the London Road and on the edge of Savernake Forest. It was a long low pleasant collection of buildings and if you took a walk in that part of the forest, you would see patients in beds outside for fresh air was regarded an a universal panacea. For many years the matron of the hospital was a very outstanding woman named Miss Lavington and under her direction, Savernake became a model for cottage hospitals. While I was never a patient there, we visited friends there from time to time, making the long trek up a steep hill to reach the hospital.

When my sister left school, Mother decided it woul be good to find out if she would like a career in nursing so she started to work at Savernake Hospital doing hard and menial tasks for a very small wage. My mercurial and fun loving sister soon decided that there must be a better way of making a living than by emptying bedpans and the nursing experience was soon terminated. But it was enough to give me an insight into the workings of a hospital and, like May, I came to the conclusion that hospital nursing was not for me.

Minor and emergency operations were performed in the hospital by local doctors who were qualified surgeons, but most surgery was done by specialists, who visited Savernake regularly from the teaching hospitals in Oxford, Swindon, Salisbury and Reading. The specialists, who were always addressed as 'Mr.' rather than 'Dr.', were the prima donnas of the medical profession. They were greeted by the immaculately uniformed nurses drawn up in almost military precision, waited on hand, foot and finger, treated with great awe and respect by the general practitioners and regarded with fear and trepidation by their patients.

There were only a few private rooms in the hospital, most patients being in surgical or medical, men's, women's or children's wards, according to their complaints, sex and age. Each ward was in the charge of a highly qualified nurse known as Sister and working under her were a staff of nurses and probationers, distinguished by the colour of their uniform and type of headgear, as well as the type of work assigned to them.

After living for thirty-five years in the United States, I am grateful for American doctors and hospitals, though whenever I have been a hospital patient, I have missed the cool, crisp, calm efficiency of the British nurse, who carries on in the highest traditions of Florence Nightingale.

In addition to the doctors in the town and working closely with them were two middle-aged district nurses who lived in a lovely little Georgian house in the Green. Like Dr. Maurice they cycled to their cases and it was a reassuring sight to see them pedalling along in all weathers. In summer they wore their blue stiffly starched uniforms but in winter they covered them with long navy blue coats. On ceremonial occasions such as Armistice Day, they would appear in the dark blue scarlet lined cloaks of the Queen Alexandra Nursing Service – they had both served in front line hospitals during the war – and then I would be briefly overcome with a patriotic desire to become an army nurse for I thought they looked so beautiful. These nurses, who gave many years of devoted service to their profession, were towers of strength in the community, providing nursing care for old, indigent and dying people, looking after patients just discharged from hospital, delivering babies and educating new mothers in their family reponsibilities. In the twenties most babies were born at home and most were brought into the world by nurse midwives. In some families a doctor's service might be contracted for, but usually a doctor was called only if difficulties arose. I think women preferred midwives – perhaps feeling more comfortable with one of their own sex. It was in the thirties that women began to go to hospital to have their babies. Prior to that time, there was little pre-natal care and pregnancy was regarded as a condition that should be hidden as long as possible. On 21 October 1977, my grandson, Samuel Day Wharton, was born in Junction City, Oregon. He was born at home and delivered by a midwife. The wheel had come full circle.

Both doctors and nurses adjusted their fees according to the means of their patients and some of it was delivered free. My mother was always billed by the doctor and she was always very prompt with payment. Once after a prolonged siege of illness she received a bill for five pounds, a large sum of money in those days. She was forced to pay it in installments which was a source of considerable embarrassment to her.

As far back as the 1920s British schools provided rudimentary but regular medical care. A nurse came to the school every month to examine children for diseases and conditions associated with dirt – scabies, impetigo, lice. Such things were rampant among the poor, a result of large families and poor living conditions. They posed a threat of contagion to those of us who were kept scrupulously clean. Every Friday night Mother would go through our hair with a tooth comb and then shampoo it thoroughly. Once she found a nit in May's long hair which precipitated washings and treatments of crisis proportions. After that May's hair was cut short and we were never allowed to wear it long again. A doctor came once a year to schools for routine medical examinations, with any abnormality referred to a practicing doctor, and also a dentist came who filled and extracted teeth as he saw fit. There was no charge for these services which were a boon to the poor, as indigent, undernourished children were recommended for and received free milk and other nutritional supplements.

The elementary schools did an admirable job in trying to raise standards of cleanliness and personal hygiene. We had to show our hands daily to the teachers and girls with dirty hands or untidy hair were sent out to remedy the matter. Neatness in dress was encouraged and we were always told that though many of us could not afford new clothes it did not cost anything to be neat and tidy. Every Friday the whole school was inspected by the headmistress and at this assembly two banners were awarded. The first went to the class which had the best attendance, but the second, rather tattered and torn, was awarded to the neatest class of girls. It bore the legend 'Cleanliness is next to Godliness.'

Chapter XXXIV

Like all English children of our generation, we played certain games ritually and seasonally. After the long winter when most of our activities were perforce confined to the house, it was the spinning top that appeared as if by magic on Good Friday. The tops were brightly coloured wooden cylinders about four inches long, pointed at one end and ridged where the whip was wound round. The tops were kept spinning by lashes from a whip and I have seen tops lifted by the whip and transferred many feet through the air to continue humming and spinning when they reached the ground. Some children were extremely clever at this – I never was, but the humming of tops and the cracking of the whips was the general signal to England's child population that spring had arrived. The spinning tops were followed in quick succession by skipping ropes (girls only), hoops, large wooden circles propelled by short sticks, the trick being to keep up with the hoop and not let it get away and then balls, which reigned supreme all summer long. Balls ranged from large brightly coloured hollow balls to small rubber balls and tennis balls. Balls were bounced on pavements, banged against buildings, thrown by hand or hit with a racquet or cricket bat and where two or three children gathered together, a pick up game of cricket, rounders or stool ball would develop. My mother hated the ball season – the endless rhythmic bouncing got on her nerves and she considered them dangerous, as indeed they were on the narrow twisty English roads with their non-existent or inadequate pavements and traffic getting heavier by the year. The early summer always brought a rise in accidents involving children who dashed into the street after a ball. But balls stayed with us all the summer and well on into autumn when footballs appeared and infinite varieties of games and ball drills based on soccer took over. Fads like yo-yos and hula hoops came and went but the tops, ropes, hoops and balls came in their appointed season year in year out. Some games, especially ones involving skipping ropes, were played to nonsense rhymes and jingles which were handed down for generations, their original meanings lost in antiquity.

When I was at the Grammar School, the girls played hockey and netball in the winter and tennis in the summer, while the boys enjoyed football in the cold weather and cricket in summer. Tennis was the only game I ever enjoyed and the only one in which I progressed beyond the 'duffer' stage. I neither had the physique or the courage for hockey. For years Thursday afternoons were given over to games. The playing fields were quite a distance from the school and we walked the one-half mile or so along the London Road and up Buck Lane in crocodile fashion. I always hoped it would rain hard (a gentle drizzle never deterred us) – but in hockey I learned to endure the cold, the mud, the shouted rebukes of teachers and team mates and the occasional crack on the shin with stoic calm and a stiff upper lip. I was equally inept at netball – a watered down version of "American basketball" which was played on the asphalt courts at school. In summer since we did not have enough tennis courts to accommodate all the girls, we also played rounders and stoolball. Both the latter are old games dating from Tudor and Stuart times and are rudimentary forms of cricket and baseball. Our physical education also encompassed dancing, folk dancing, country dancing and quadrilles and lancers, the figure dances which preceded ballroom dancing at balls and parties.

But the mainstay of outdoor activity during childhood was going for walks. As we grew older, weekends and holidays would find us taking off on the inevitable walk and without benefit of watch, turning up at the right time for dinner or tea or in the long summer evenings at bedtime. Perhaps our stomachs told us when to get home and often we were within sight or sound of a church clock – but Mother expected us to be prompt and we were rarely late. For our walks we had a choice of forest, downland, meadowland or riverside and we got to know the environs of the town quite thoroughly. We would tell Mother where we thought we were going and take off either by ourselves or with some of our friends for several hours. Sometimes, we would take a picnic tea into Savernake Forest, sometimes wander around Preshute Churchyard reading the gravestones and speculating on inscriptions such as 'Dear Little Dickie' who died in 1900 aged four. For some weeks we played almost daily in a huge tree trunk which had fallen across the River Kennet. Chopping Knife, Treacle Bolly, Folly Farm, Four Mile Clump, Rabley Woods and other exotically named lanes and beauty spots were all waiting for us. Mother had warned us never to speak to strangers and during our perambulations, we never encountered any untoward behaviour. Though homeless tramps wandered the countryside, we gave them a wide berth. If they came to the house, Mother would give them tea and bread and bid them a quick adieu. Cows presented the only challenge and I was never comfortable when I shared a field with them even though they went on placidly munching grass or chewing their cuds. There was some small danger of encountering a bull though usually he would be enclosed in a field barred by a gate bearing the warning 'Beware of the Bull.' As children, we never owned bicycles and it was not until after I was teaching that I owned or rode one.

On our perambulations, we would often gather wildflowers and bring them home to Mother. The pale yellow primroses came in March and were followed by the bluebells – wild hyacinths that carpeted the woods in their deep purplish blue. As we picked them we exposed their naked white stems and they were flowers that never looked well out of their natural habitat. The earliest of all the wildflowers were the gentle nodding snowdrops which could be gathered by the handful from among the graves in Preshute Churchyard in late January and February. The wild anemone or windflower was pretty and dainty but we learned from experience that it very quickly faded as did the bright scarlet poppy which grew in the cornfields in high summer. When white daisies and blue cornflowers were added to the red poppies, the fields of golden harvest assumed something of a patriotic air. We liked to pick cowslips and when we were near the river, we would find shiny yellow kingcups and the pale lavender cuckoo flower. The delicate pink dog-rose bloomed in the hedgerows in July and its sharp thorns protected it to some extent from our depredations. In late September or October, we ranged the hedges in search of blackberries and hazelnuts and late summer's heavy dews brought mushrooms, if we could wake up early enough to gather them. These were the finest mushrooms I have ever eaten. If large, Mother would fry them with bacon, if in the button stage she would gently simmer them in a delicate cream sauce and serve them on toast. We never worried about confusing mushrooms and toadstools – whole fields of snowy mushroom umbrellas with their delicate flesh pink linings were there for the picking and were not infiltrated with any other form of mycological life.

Autumn brought us another plaything – conkers – the fruit of the horse chestnut tree. From out of its green thorny outer covering we would prise the shiny nut, tie it on a string and battle with our friends likewise armed with conkers.

Our playmates were mostly girls from the neighbourhood with whom we walked to and from school. My sister had many friends and was given to crushes on people which began and ended suddenly and rarely lasted long. I had less friends but tended to keep them longer and it was rather a traumatic part of changing school when I left some old friends and had to make new ones in a strange school. Mother liked us to be together on our walks and expeditions but did not insist as I think she felt it was good for us to develop separate interests and friends. There were often new children coming into our neighbourhood and May was quick to get to know them. One, a girl named Nancy Fidler, I remember very vividly. Her father, a soldier, had brought his family home from India and we regarded her almost as an exotic creature from outer space. Playing at her house once, she approached May saying, "Open your mouth and shut your eyes and you will find a great surprise." As this was a favourite way of giving a friend a sweet, May did just that and Nancy popped into her mouth a heaping spoonful of dry Colman's mustard. I thought May would choke to death and I think it very fortunate that she did not. After that I viewed Nancy with deep mistrust.

When I had been a couple of years at the Grammar School, a family with all kinds of romantic connotations, arrived in Marlborough from San Francisco. Their mother had married an American Soldier in World War I and had gone to America where five children had been born to them, and he had worked as a newspaperman before succumbing to a disability incurred during the war. Mrs. Chubbuck was the daughter of an elderly couple named Russell, he, a prosperous tailor and haberdasher who catered almost entirely to the exclusive college trade. When her husband died, the widow and five children returned to Marlborough. They were a delightful family and the eldest, a wide mouthed, freckle-faced, curly-haired girl named Mary came into my class. She was two years older than the rest of us, good at games and soon became popular with everyone. I remember being envious of her beautiful handwriting – she had been taught the Palmer Method in common use in U.S. schools then and for many years. The three younger sisters and one brother were all very attractive, talented children. They had not been long in Marlborough when their mother became ill and after a long siege in the hospital she remained permanently lame. Mary became the surrogate mother. While we did not think of it at the time, I have thought since what an upheaval in the lives of their grandparents this family must have brought. Mary became a nurse, trained at Middlesex Hospital, a happy choice of career, but at the beginning of the Second World War as American citizens, she and her brother and sisters all returned to the United States. Years later I saw a newspaper clipping in England about her work as a United States Army nurse. Mary and I were good though never close friends. I found much in her that I desired to emulate.

My closest friend at Marlborough Grammar School was Molly Trollope. She rode the train in every day from Woodborough. She was short and plump, with the prettiest curly hair, rose petal complexion and a delightful tip-tilted nose. We shared many interests both in and out of school.

Another good friend was Gwyn Burgess, whose father owned a thriving fruit and flower business in Marlborough. Her mother was a championship golfer and was often away from home leaving Gwyn in charge of her little brother who was some 12 years younger than she was. Gwyn became an excellent student, with French her major subject. For several years she exchanged summer visits with a French boy named Jean, whom we all liked very much. She went to Oxford and took an honours degree in French. In addition she was an outstanding athlete, being an especially fine hockey player. She was very fond of my mother and visited her whenever she was in Marlborough. Molly and I envied her her athletic ability and also her piano playing talent. She became a French teacher in Bournemouth and some years ago in New Jersey I met an English girl who had been one of her pupils. Unfortunately I have lost touch with her, though I remember her fondly and hear news of her occasionally from her older brother Don who took over the family business and still resides in Marlborough.

During the long cold wet days and evenings of winter, we resorted to card games such as 'Snap' and 'Old Maid' to while away the time. Each Christmas brought us a new board game and we had a lot of fun with 'Ludo' and 'Snakes and Ladders' and an ancient game requiring some skill, called 'Halma'. We were limited in our game playing by virtue of being only two, but sometimes Mother and Dad would join in and then happy and secure, we had a lot of fun.

To our sorrow we had little experience as children of winter sports such as skating, tobogganing, or even building a snowman. In those years there seemed a dearth of snow. Sometimes, it would be snowing when we went to bed, but by morning it would have turned to rain and slush and our hopes were dashed. Perhaps weather does indeed go in cycles and snow seemed to pass us by for many years. Father would often talk of bitterly cold snowy winters when he was a boy and he would tell how all the young people in the village would go skating on the canal. Mother too would tell of struggling to school through snowy lanes. We had an old print at home showing a stagecoach stuck in snowdrifts near Amesbury on Salisbury Plain, and I read of the bitter Devon winter experienced by Jan Ridd in *Lorna Doone*. But the worse weather we got was bitter cold in January and February, when frozen pipes could wreak havoc with plumbing and when the penetrating east wind blowing off the landmass of the Eurasian continent would dry and chap our cheeks and lips, and inflict our hands and feet with the curse of chilblains. Weather like that was 'neither good for man nor beast' and we longed for the return of the balmy west wind even though that usually meant rain.

It was not until 1939, the first year of Second World War, that we got a good old-fashioned snowy winter. By that time there was nothing 'good' about it – I was no longer a child and the many weeks of snow and bitter cold merely aggravated and intensified the miseries of wartime winter. I remember seeing the British Tommies slipping and sliding on icy streets in their unaccustomed hobnailed government issue boots. Many pulled old socks over them to gain a little traction and it was rumoured that some padded their trouser seats with newspapers to cushion their frequent falls. There were more bad winters to come straining further already stretched fuel resources, snarling road and rail traffic, causing accidents and generally adding to the troubles of soldiers and civilians alike.

Chapter XXXV

My parents had many friends and acquaintances who brought colour
and interest into our lives. Father always attracted people better
educated and in a better position than he was by virtue of his many
talents and abilities, and people seemed to like Mother and seek her
out because she was calm and quiet, a good listener and always ready
with commonsense, advice and practical help. It seemed to me that
my own children never felt much affinity for our friends or vice
versa, yet Mother and Dad's friends were vital forces and influences
in our lives. When we were invited out to tea – the hub of social
entertainment at that time – we not only enjoyed the delicious food,
but the company of cultured people living in greater luxury than we
were. They for their part always seemed glad to see the two little
girls who were never left at home but accompanied their parents on
all social occasions.

One good friend who often asked us to tea was the wife of an
official in the local branch of Lloyd's Bank. She was a plump blonde
lady and I thought she was very pretty and admired the frilly pastel
hued clothes she favoured. When we first knew them, she and her
husband lived in a flat over a shop in one of the Tudor buildings in
the High Street. It had an enormous panelled living room and all
kinds of nooks and crannies – just the place for ghosts, I thought,
though this idea was negated to some extent by the soft comfortable
furniture covered in flowered chintz. They had no children, but kept
a cat which used to go quite wild every evening, tearing around the
room emitting unearthly shrieks and clawing drapes and furniture. I
was frightened of the cat and he rather spoiled my visits. But when
they moved to a house near us, the cat was replaced by a lovely
spaniel dog, which we were permitted to walk whenever we wished
to do so. It was always a great treat when their niece Marjorie visited
them, from Bournemouth. She had many advantages over us and
we were a bit envious of her and a little in awe of her too. She went
to a boarding school and had the clipped speech and bearing that we
lacked. She was fond of both horses and dogs, very athletic, stockily

built and rather plain but we all got along well and her visits were welcomed for several years.

Occasionally we were invited to tea by my father's employer's housekeeper. This lady, not much younger than my parents, was an old friend and Father had been instrumental in getting her her job. Mr. Hooper, a bachelor, had built a charming house west of town on the Bath Road. To get there meant a two-mile walk which we could only undertake if the weather was fine. The road there led us through the town, past many of the college buildings, past Preshute Church and along an avenue of chestnut trees where in the fall, we would hunt for 'conkers'. Miss Hutchins always had a lovely tea for us and we liked the beautiful garden and the house which though not large, was delightfully appointed and furnished.

Yet another friend who added considerable interest to our lives was a lady named, Mrs. Ireland. She was tiny and blonde and always wore pince nez glasses. With her husband, a tall gangling individual with a compulsive repetitive speech habit – they were oddly matched – she rented a couple of rooms near us. She had arrived in Marlborough some months before in the last stages of pregnancy but had lost the baby – an eleven pound boy. She attributed the baby's death to the failure of the doctor to arrive in time to save it. She was in a bad state of depression when she first began to talk to Mother, and the two became firm friends, Mother obviously helping her over a very rough patch in her life.

Her story was an interesting one. She had been married before, when very young, to a sea captain, old enough to be her father and had travelled on his ship with him for several years and had visited most of the major ports of the world. Then tired of travelling, she elected to stay in England, but bored, lonely and restless, took a job as a nurse in a hospital near Newcastle. There she met and fell madly in love with a young electrician with whom she subsequently ran away. It appears now unlikely that they were married at the time we first knew them or at the time her child was born.

She took a great fancy to me, spoiling me outrageously and giving me many interesting gifts – things she had picked up in her travels – an ivory backed hairbrush with whalebone bristles, a silver hand mirror, the back embossed with Sir Joshua Reynolds 'Heads of Angels', a Russian icon and a picture of Christ's crucifixion in an oval heavily carved frame. She gave Mother some purple silk cushion covers embroidered with gold dragons, which she had bought in China. The couple were short of cash and she was in the midst of litigation about money with her first husband. She had obviously been used to a great deal more money than her present husband earned as a garage mechanic. She then became ill with back trouble and spent many months in Salisbury Infirmary. When released she had to wear a special corset that held her absolutely rigid. It looked to me like a suit of armour.

Eventually, the couple moved permanently to Salisbury and of necessity, we saw less of them but I was often invited to Salisbury to stay with her. Their money situation seemed resolved for they had a lovely house there and Salisbury is one of the most delightful of all English cities. Desperately unhappy that she had no children, she finally adopted a boy. I saw her once after I was married and she was at my mother's funeral, though I was not. I remember her with great affection – her travels fascinated me, I responded to her interest in me, and I always felt her story epitomized the saying, 'the world well lost for love.'

Father through his beekeeping, also made friends with an artist who lived with his family in an old cottage extensively modernised, in a village called Grafton. A big bearded handsome man, he was married to a woman with a strikingly beautiful face, but who was overweight to the point of obesity. They had two darkly beautiful children, a boy named Merlin, who became a Cambridge educated doctor, and a girl named Naomi. I was about sixteen at the time and becoming quite shapely and I was the target of the artist's admiring though lascivious eye. My mother watched me like a hawk and made sure I was never alone with him. He was quite a fine oil painter and his wife was a skilled potter. They could be said to belong to the intelligentsia and they had many Bohemian friends who visited them in droves from London. While my mother did not approve of them or their friends, Father was fascinated by them – I think he would like to have been part of such a set. One group from London persuaded my father to get together a large assortment of wooden articles – marquetry pictures, bowls, trinkets, etc. which they would sell at a commission in the city. Father worked long and hard to get together a fine collection. Mother packed it all and it was shipped to London. He never received any payment from them in spite of letters and phone calls. Mother, of course, was furious, saying "I told you so" in no uncertain terms. Another young couple we met at their house invited me to spend a weekend with them in Soho when I was at college in London. I did so, but found myself in a very avant-garde Bohemian group. Nothing untoward occurred but I felt on unfamiliar ground and dangerous territory and refused all further invitations from them.

Our artist friend collapsed and died of a heart attack while on a visit to Belgium just before the war and shortly afterwards his wife and family left Grafton. They showed me a facet of life I had hitherto not been exposed to, lent me books from their extensive library and gave me some small exposure to art.

Though Father, like my sister, was prone to make friends quickly but often not keep them very long, he did have some friends that he had known for many years. One, a man named Bill Ball, worked in the village of Upavon. With his plump red-haired wife Emmy, he lived in a pretty old thatched cottage with the proverbial English garden redolent with lavender, mignonette and pinks. Dad had met him many years previously when they were both young chauffeurs together. The Balls, to Emmy's sorrow, had no children and they were always delighted when we visited them. Mrs. Ball would fold us to her ample bosom, then bring out tea, lemonade and all manner of good things to eat – she had been in service as a cook.

On one of my last visits to England to see my sister during her long illness, my brother-in-law took me for a ride around Wiltshire's village and we stopped on the spur of the moment in Upavon to see the Balls. Emmy, her bright red hair faded to a nondescript grey, and her firm plumpness reduced to sagging folds, took one look at me – a middle-aged smartly dressed American woman – and said in her broad Wiltshire "Why 'tis Vrank's girl!" Her eyes filled with tears and she enfolded me in the old embrace. Then sending a little neighbour boy off to find her husband, she poured tea from the ever ready pot on the hob and produced as of old, her scones and homemade jam.

Chapter XXXVI

Into the safe, confined and limited environment of childhood some knowledge of sin, evil and death inevitably crept in. As children we had very clear-cut, black and white ideas of good and evil – only as we grew older did confusing grey areas arise. Our thoughts on sin and wickedness, such as they were, were introduced and formulated by the Church of England catechism which we learned by heart, and studied regularly in school and Sunday School. Our moral values were largely caught from Mother and Father who were honest, straightforward caring individuals who taught us by example and precept.

Our town's population experienced its share of death, disease and tragedy. A muffled peal of bells announced a death to the community and after the peal came the sad tolling – one for each year of the deceased's life. We would count and speculate as to who had been taken from our midst. Our next door neighbour, a youngish man, died of pneumonia leaving a widow and two little girls. A little younger than we were, for many years they were our constant playmates. We felt their sorrow keenly and for a while we were much afraid of losing one of our parents. His body lay in his house until the funeral and during those days we had to remain very quiet with the shades on the windows drawn down. His corpse was taken on a hand bier to the church for the funeral service and interment.

One of our playmates, a boy a little older than we were, died of diabetes which claimed him with lightning speed. Mother, inexact and misinformed for once, explained that there were three kinds of diabetes, eating, drinking and sugar. Of the three, she said, sugar was the worst and always fatal. This threw me into paroxyms of fear that I would contract the disease. But of all the illnesses, cancer was the one most dreaded. There appeared to be some stigma attached to it and it was never discussed openly, only in whispers and half veiled references. Once during a visit to the local hospital, we saw in the woman's ward a pale red-haired girl of about thirteen who, we learned, was dying of cancer. Her pallor, made worse by dark freckles and sunken eyes, made a profound impression on me. A few weeks later I read her obituary in the local paper. Her name, I remember, was Betty Saunders and she was thirteen. As mentioned before, our music teacher had to go to London for a mastectomy, a word unused and unknown to us at that time. She was a close friend of Mother's and from their whispered confidences, we learned a little about her illness.

My first experience of death came at age four when my grandmother died. I have a dim recollection of her, thin and gaunt with black circles around her deep-set eyes sitting up in bed in her tiny house in Erlestoke. My father and mother were almost late for her funeral and I heard my mother tell many times how my father hit ninety miles per hour in the Hudson touring car he drove on the straight Roman road across the downs between Beckhampton and Devizes. We were left in charge of Mrs. Garside. She took us for a walk by the river along a lane called Stoney Bridges and I picked a bunch of shiny yellow kingcups from the marshy watermeadows of the River Kennet.

When I was thirteen or fourteen a family death hit us very hard. One of my mother's younger sisters had moved from the village of Potterne near Devizes to Urchfont, where she and her husband kept a public house – the Lamb. I doubt that Americans have any idea of the hard unremitting labour involved in keeping a country pub. Day in, day out, the house has to be open for regular license hours 10 a.m. to 2 p.m., 6 p.m. to 10 or 11 p.m., the only exception being New Year's Day, with slightly shorter periods on Sundays. My aunt's husband was a cattle dealer, here, there and everywhere in the rural district of Devizes, so that the burden of running the pub, raising two children, looking after a large garden and caring for a motley assortment of animals fell upon this delicate little woman. She literally worked herself to death.

One Sunday we arrived at Urchfont for, we thought, a happy afternoon visit, to find my aunt in bed with pneumonia. For the first time in our lives, Mother sent Dad, May and myself home without her while she stayed to nurse her sister. All to no avail, for after an anxious week of round-the-clock nursing for my mother and of waiting (no phone, remember) for us, Aunt Nellie died. I was heartbroken. She was my favourite aunt and my godmother and I had spent many vacations with her. Mother would not permit us to go to her funeral, feeling it would be too emotionally draining for us. In order to assuage my sorrow, I went to the local cinema and saw a movie called 'Waltz Time' about Vienna in its heyday. To this day, any picture of old Vienna, any snatch of a Strauss waltz, will bring back my grief and I suffer a sharp pang not only for the loss of a dear aunt but for the futility of her life. But perhaps one cannot call it futility when she is remembered so clearly fifty years later and 3,000 miles away and when she always exhibited and comunicated a zest for life in spite of a hard and unrewarding environment.

Another tragedy that hurt very much was the death in childbirth of a twenty-three year-old farmer's wife. Phyllis's husband was a prosperous farmer living in Burbage and both were members of prominent and comparatively affluent farming families. My father had met Bill, found common interests with him and we began to exchange visits. I was sixteen or seventeen at the time and Phyllis not much older. She was tiny, sweet and unsophisticated, pretty in a shy modest way. She was madly in love with her husband and he with her, though she was considerably younger than he was. He was tall, dark and saturnine in appearance, slow moving, slow speaking, but a fine businessman, well read, and intelligent. Their farmhouse, large, commodious, comfortably furnished and set well back from the main road was sheltered by the edge of Salisbury Plain. I spent a lot of time there during holidays and weekends. It was a happy meeting of two girls, one intellectually inclined but uncertain of the future, the other happily settled in a traditional role. They were delighted at the prospect of the baby and the pregnancy went well. But in the local hospital, the child was born dead and Phyllis died shortly afterwards.

Hers was the only funeral I ever attended in England. It was a classic English scene – the old grey church, a beautiful summer day, birds singing, a heartbroken husband, grieving family and friends, the surpliced rector intoning the age-old words of the funeral service as the young mother and her child were committed to a common grave.

Chapter XXXVII

In my day, in the class to which we belonged, parents, especially mothers, were very ambitious for their children. For boys, the avenue to a better life lay through education, but this was closed to many girls through lack of funds, especially when there were boys in the family. However, there was always the chance that a girl would make a 'good' marriage and mothers concentrated on making their daughters attractive to look at and trained them to the best of their ability in the housewifely arts. The pre-marriage years in families with daughters were anxious ones, however, for a good marriage was a gamble and the potential alternatives of a shotgun wedding or, much worse, an illegitimate baby, presented the ultimate disgrace.

We were completely uninformed on the facts of life. Neither parents or schools made any attempt to enlighten us. I well remember the horrible shock of the menarche and how my mother, flushed and embarrassed, said she thought I would have learned about it at school. In fairness to my mother I am sure she agonized for many months over whether to tell or not to tell. Even when I had digested something of my own physiological changes I still knew nothing about boys and babies. I was not alone in my ignorance. In the 'brainy' set of which I was part, at school, we simply did not talk about sex, and, though we read books like *Tess of the d'Urbervilles* and *Hatter's Castle* both dealing with the defloration of innocence and an ultimate baby, we drew no parallels and made no application to ourselves. I even read Radcliffe Hall's classic story of lesbianism, *The Well of Loneliness*, without having the faintest idea of what it was about. At the age of nineteen in college, in common with my contemporaries, we anxiously awaited a much touted lecture by the college doctor on the facts of life. While she gave a graphic description of the birth process, she made no mention of the part the father played in how the baby got there and I remember the disappointment in which most of us seemed to share.

Long afterwards, teaching in Glen Rock, every year we used to show a film entitled 'Growing Up' to the fifth and sixth grade girls and their mothers followed by a discussion and question and answer period. While it was the school nurse's responsibilty to present the programme, somehow it became my assignment. I performed it, I believe, with authority, objectivity, some sense of humour and a private feeling of vindication for my mother's long ago sin of omission. Hopefully, I have helped a few little American girls avoid the shock and embarrassment that I encountered through ignorance and a false sense of modesty.

Growing up in a two-girl family, our contacts with boys were nil. Our closest friends, the Garsides, had three boys, the oldest of whom was four years younger than I, and we saw our boy cousins, also younger than we were, only on rare occasions. The elementary school I attended was for girls only and though Marlborough Grammar School was co-educational, it seemed the aim and object of the authorities to keep boys and girls as completely separated as possible. We entered school through separate doors and were segregated in the classrooms by a wide aisle. Socializing, even to the extent of walking to school together, was frowned upon and the only purely social contact we had with the opposite sex was at the annual social held by each house of 'set'.

From a shy, mousey and, I might add, prolonged adolescence, I grew into a tall girl with a well-proportioned figure, small feet and hands and slender legs. My looks, such as they were, were typically English – perhaps wholesome would best describe them. My features were regular, teeth white and straight, the whole high-lighted by the beautiful pink and white complexion which is the heritage of so many English girls, product of damp climate and cold houses. My hair, then as now, was my worst feature. Baby fine and straight and a nondescript blonde, the harsh permanents of the day plus unremitting nightly care helped it out to some extent. My dear school friend, Molly Trollope, her own head a mass of bobbing curls, used to console me by saying my hair was fine like silk and the colour of honey – in view of my negative feelings about honey hardly the happiest of analogies. Molly married a New Zealander during the war and my only contact with her since our schooldays is an annual exchange of letters. Hers, for me is one of the highlights of the Christmas season and I feel sure the same is true of mine to her.

There were some in the town who considered me pretty but I always felt eclipsed by my sister's vivid brunette looks. I lacked her magnetism for the opposite sex and envied her the ease with which she related to men and boys.

When local girls were sixteen or seventeen, they began to attend the frequent dances held, mostly in aid of various charities, at the Town Hall. Young men, usually somewhat older than the girls, came from the town itself and the surrounding villages in search of a dancing partner, or mild flirtation. Many a romance begun in the Town Hall led to the altar at St. Mary's Church hard by. Indeed my own did, though my bridegroom was not a local man, but a United States Army officer.

Most of the young men we met at these local dances in the thirties were well-mannered gentlemanly types, mostly farmers or in farmer connected jobs, with not much money, and very lucky if they owned a car. Mother and Dad always warned us against going in cars with young men and against drinking. I am afraid both rules, we broke.

A British institution that made little impact on us as children was the 'pub'. My father, a teetotaller, never visited a public house, though I am sure he would have enjoyed the conversation, bonhomie and camaraderie. He resented the time he spent waiting for his employer outside the pubs and hotels – time which became longer with each passing year. As we grew older and began to meet young men he was adamant that we stay out of pubs and hotels, saying that to be seen in them was bad for the reputation and that drinking would lead to 'trouble'. I obeyed him to some extent, but often on a date there was nowhere else to go when the weather was too cold or wet to walk and we had already been to the local cinema. My sister defied his prohibitions quite blatantly. I, being more circumspect, older when I began to date and away from Marlborough more than she was, tried to keep his rules and felt a sense of guilt when I broke them. I did learn from him to drink very moderately and this habit I have retained. From his scenes with my sister I also learned that to forbid something dictatorially is the surest way to drive a person to do what you are trying to keep them from. May's wild escapades and frequent romances exacerabated my father and worried my mother for many years and it was not until after the war that she settled down into a rather humdrum marriage.

When I was about eighteen, I had a shortlived romance with the oldest son of a wealthy family which owned many acres of rich farmland in Pewsey Vale. My normally sensible mother, scenting a possible marriage, was very happy and appeared quite willing to sacrifice my educational future, though she must have realised I would have no stomach for point to points, or fox hunting, nor the strength, stamina and know-how for running a huge farm establishment.

I liked the young men I met in Marlborough and at college and in my early days of teaching. Only one of these touched me deeply. I met him in Marlborough and continued to date him in London where he was at the Royal Naval College at Greenwich. Marriage was never mentioned – before the war, it was out of the question for a young naval officer who did not possess a private income. Late in 1938, he was posted overseas and became an early casualty of the war. Tall, dark, romantically handsome and with a poet's soul, I remember him with poignancy and affection.

Most of the boys I went to school with and those I dated in the halcyon days before the war, were destined to fight for their country and were often sent to the uttermost ends of the earth in 1939 and 1940. In many cases soldiers from Free France, Poland, Norway, Canada, Australia, New Zealand and most of all from the United States, fell in love with and married the girls the British boys had left behind.

Chapter XXXVIII

I have sung my parents' praises and I loved them dearly. I do not mean to detract from them in any way when I make two criticisms.

They were after all the products of their age and of their social circumstances and these imposed some limitations, especially when viewed in the light of today and all we have learned about child rearing and psychology.

First of all my mother hated what she called 'mess'. We lived in a small house with a small living room where all the living had to go on for about eight months of the year because with its open fireplace, it was the only heated area. So we could never play with clay or plasticine, we could draw but not paint because we might spill the water necessary for the latter. On the rare occasions when after much begging, she allowed me to paint the fear of spilling the water caused inhibition. Thus I developed a fear of artistic self-expression, did poorly in art in school and avoided it in college. It was while teaching in Glen Rock that I discovered I could not only draw and paint myself, but could bring out the artistic talent of my students. In addition to art lessons I found I could develop art projects from other subjects such as social studies and literature, could present children's work strikingly and working together with my pupils, developed wall displays and murals, some purely artistic, some arising from the learning disciplines. Since retirement, I have become a watercolourist.

Mother would rarely permit us to have playmates in the house. Only on birthdays or as a very special treat could we bring a friend home to tea. When I made friends with Molly at the Grammar School, I sometimes used to stay with her in Woodborough where her father was the village schoolmaster. On a few occasions Mother permitted me to invite her to our house and then I was very happy but I knew Mother did not like the extra work, having her routine interrupted and I also knew she was embarrassed by our lack of a bathroom and other niceties.

The other legacy on the wrong side of the ledger was a slight though real sense of social inferiority. We were poor and my father's employment, at the beck and call of an auctioneer, could not be considered to have much status. This contributed to a sense of insecurity and lack of self-confidence which has been with me most of my life. A lot of it has disappeared or become submerged in my life in the United States thanks to an intelligent, understanding, socially secure husband, a successful teaching career and fortune which has smiled on me.

The Green and 7th Wilts War Memorial opposite our house, before the memorial was moved in the nineteen twenties. The man in the right centre is my father.

With cousins, dogs and sister at the Lamb Inn in Urchfont about 1928. I am wearing the Marlborough Grammar School blazer.

My father the Beekeeper.

My father outside his workshop in Angel Yard with our dog Mick

Above: Savernake Forest Woodcraft

Left: My sister Frances May in Savernake Forest

Right: My sister, Frances May

Left: The author taken while a student
at Whitelands College in 1937

Above: Sergeant Biggs of the Home
Guard in 1941

Left: My father in 1949

King George VI and Queen Elizabeth when they visited Marlborough 19 March 1948. They are pictured at the Town Hall and are
in the company of Alderman and Mrs. James Duck, Mayor and
Mayoress of Marlborough

The author today in her home in Chapel Hill. The painting is done by Canadian artist Victor Sharpe of Vancouver, the author's first cousin.

Chapter XXXIX

My parents had both been in domestic service and my father's twenty-year job driving for an auctioneer had an element of service about it. In the decade after the Great War people who had been in service were somewhat looked down on, while those who continued in it or wanted to do so were held in even lower esteem. Much has been written about the lot of the servant in the nineteenth and early twentieth centuries and the enchanting television series 'Upstairs, Downstairs' examined the master–servant relationship thoroughly and thoughtfully. Though the Industrial Revolution had begun its demise, it was the war which brought to a close the long era in which many people worked for a few, often on huge estates and in a hierarchy that had its roots in the feudal system of the Middle Ages. After 1918, many masters had lost their money or were taxed so heavily that it was no longer feasible to maintain so extravagant a life-style and in addition many servants had lost their zest for service and were looking for employment in the many new areas the war had opened up.

Few people today realise that, prior to 1914, for the country lad or lass who left the village school at twelve or thirteen, the next step was employment at one of the 'big' houses in the vicinity – every village boasted several. It was a natural progression in life, young people following in their parents' footsteps and in company with their peers.

Service had several advantages. Young people were fed, clothed, housed, protected, taught to perform certain duties well and conscientiously. The pay was low, but it was free and clear and many a young servant was able to contribute much of her small pittance, to the family back home. There were also possibilities for advancement in service for the able and dedicated worker. To be the head housekeeper, cook, butler or gamekeeper took much ability and managerial skill and were positions of great respect. People doing similar work today would be likely to have a college degree in their particular field.

For the girl especially service was the easy, often the only, answer as she grew old enough for work. Boys had more to choose from – the army, the navy, farm labouring, emigration for the adventure minded to distant outposts of the Empire. Generally speaking too, boys had a better education from which to launch a future career. Even so many village lads became gardeners, footmen, gamekeepers or grooms at a 'big' house, often remaining their entire lives working for the same family. Families felt that in service, a girl was looked after and taught skills that would be useful after marriage and in addition responsibility for her welfare was lifted from the shoulders of her parents and laid upon those of her employers. What else was available or could be better for the minimally educated girl before World War I.

Service however was no sinecure. A boy or girl had to perform well or face dismissal. Ruby in 'Upstairs, Downstairs' would not have lasted long in real life. Though the work was long and arduous, pay low and time off short, most young people accepted it cheerfully as their lot in life – as it had been the lot of their parents before them – their job in the society into which they had not had the good fortune to be born rich or noble. They had had the Church of England catechism drummed into them from their earliest years in school and had learnt by heart the telling passage – 'to learn and labour truly to get mine own living and to do my duty in that state of life unto which it has pleased God to call me.'

My father, I am sure, made a mistake when he entered private service, though by doing so he determined the course of his life and mine. Gifted as he was mechanically and artistically, with experience in barge building and an apprenticeship to boot in the Daimler Motor works, he should have remained in industry. But to a village boy with a love of the country, it was an alluring prospect to become a chauffeur – because of its newness the plum of service jobs. Wealthy landowners were on the lookout for trained drivers and mechanics, the pay was good and what could be more appealing to an adventurous young man than to travel, at the wheel of a fine car, the highways and byways of Britain from Land's End to John O'Groats? But the war ended that dream as it did so many others. From 1914 to 1918, the government trained men by the thousands to drive and maintain motor vehicles of all types in France and in 1918 mechanics and drivers were as redundant as pilots in 1945.

My mother had a rather unusual experience in service. When she had to go to work at fourteen because of the sudden death of her father, it was the clergyman at Great Cheverell who buried her father, who found a place for her in his household. Some country parsons possessed of private means and being incumbents of well-endowed livings, were able to live in a style much like that of the local squire and other gentry. Though Mother did not stay there long, it was a pleasant introduction to service and while there she made one very good friend with whom she maintained a close relationship for the rest of her life. This lady, head parlourmaid at the Rectory, who later married the blacksmith at Potterne and had one daughter, three years older than May, was known to us as 'Aunt Beat(rice)' and we spent holidays with her in her little cottage high on the cliffs of Potterne and so close to the church that when the bells rang we were almost deafened. She would regale us with tales of her service days.

Next Mother went to work as a lady's maid to a Miss Halliday, a coldly beautiful proud woman, daughter of an admiral and a spinster by choice. This lady was a hard taskmistress. She was devoted to her two dogs, one, whom Mother liked, was a Chow, the other a badly spoilt chocolate brown Pomeranian. This dog always barked furiously at Mother, who told us that whenever she passed the dog she blew gently at it sending it into paroxysms of yapping. Miss Halliday never found her out – if so, she would most likely have fired Mother on the spot without a reference. Miss Halliday, Mother said, had a beautiful head of hair, the colour of ripe corn. It was one of Mother's jobs to dress her hair every evening for dinner and sometimes she would have to do it three or four times before it was to the lady's satisfaction. Mother also had to look after Miss Halliday's clothes, laundering, pressing and mending them and she accompanied her on any trips, journeys or visits that she undertook. No wonder a suitcase packed by my mother was a work of art.

At last tired of Miss Halliday's authoritarian manner and unreasonable demands, Mother got a better paying job with a Mrs. Hume who lived at Worton Grange. Here she remained for several years until her marriage and it was in this household that her position deviated very much from the servant norm.

The Humes were a middle-aged couple of ample means and to their sorrow they were childless. Mrs. Hume had suffered several miscarriages but had never given birth to a full term live child. Mr. Hume's health was poor. He suffered from a recurrent tropical fever that he had contracted in the jungles of Panama, for he had been an engineer working on the canal. He died eventually of his illness and did not live till 1914 to see the canal opened and in use. Because of his semi-invalidism, they lived very quietly, doing little entertaining and most of his time was taken up in writing his memoirs. Mother had been hired as lady's maid to Mrs. Hume and it was an easy job after the harsh demands of Miss Halliday. It was not long before Mr. Hume discovered Mother was bright and intelligent, could read and write with fluency, spell well and gradually she spent more and more time with him writing at his dictation, anticipating his needs and becoming his general amaneunsis. Much of his writing was concerned with the Panama Canal and Mother acquired detailed knowledge of the canal which she was later to share with us.

Mother was heartbroken when Mr. Hume died – she loved and respected him very much and was grateful for the opportunity he gave her and the many doors he opened for her. She used to say he always extended to her the same courtesies that he did to his wife and other 'ladies'. His widow bought a car shortly after his death, employed a chauffeur and with Mother as her companion, toured England, always going to Devon and Cornwall in the spring and elsewhere at other seasons. Mother, like my father, enjoyed seeing so many new places and liked the life of luxury in first-class hotels, but it was a lonely time for her. Not quite a maid, not quite a companion she was suspected by the other servants and made no friends either at Worton or when travelling.

Mrs. Hume was very taken aback when Mother talked of marrying my father and promised her financial provision for life if she would stay with her and not get married. But Mother was adamant and unfortunately the two parted on somewhat less than friendly terms. She did, however, give Mother a wedding present – a bone handled Sheffield steel carving set. I have it still, the knife is the sharpest I have ever used and complete with bone handles, the set is a collector's item today. The two exchanged letters until Mrs. Hume's death, but Mother was not remembered in her will. Mother admitted that her conscience hurt because she felt she deserted Mrs. Hume. I think it goes to show how dependent upper class people often became on their servants.

In a box of old photographs that I brought from home I found a picture of Mrs. Hume which Mother had often shown me as a child. She is in court dress complete with a train, ostrich feather headress and fan, as she was presented to Queen Victoria in the 1880s. She is quite beautiful and her picture brings to mind that, as Mother used to say of her, she had not a single good feature yet the whole face was delightful. She was greatly beloved by her husband whom Mother considered a gentleman in the fullest sense of the word. As a matter of interest Mr. Hume's given name was Washington. I have often wondered if he had any connection with America's first family, but if Mother knew anything of his antecedents she never told me.

Though as children, we were somewhat ashamed of the fact that Mother was once a maid, I can see now that her service training helped make her the good housekeeper, wife and mother she was. In fact, our household was very well run and we were better brought up than the majority of our friends, most of whom were considerably more affluent than we were. Because she had lived in several fine houses, full of lovely expensive possessions, Mother acquired a love of beautiful things and a distaste for the cheap and shoddy. This ability to discriminate she passed on to us. From her employers she learned to speak well and to emulate their manners and deportment, and she taught us how to dress well, how to walk gracefully and to behave in a ladylike fashion. Within her limitations, she passed on to us the manners of the British aristocracy. Also, she learned during her working days that no matter how humble a task was, it deserved to be done to the best of the performer's ability. She preached this to us constantly, first practicing it herself, unfortunately often finding us less than apt pupils.

Though much has been written on domestic service, few people seem to perceive it as I do as a bridge, albeit a tenuous one, between the classes, the rich, noble and privileged on the one hand and the poor and deprived on the other. The aristocracy contributed something of their wealth, culture and concern to the poor but the poor returned in no small measure prosaic commonsense and practicality. Though the gulf was great it was often bridged by real friendships that grew up between master and man, mistress and maid. The role that aristocracy played in primary education in rural areas, via the parson, the lady of the manor and the squire's spinster daughters was what made the English village school superior to its American counterpart, the log cabin school. Though the landowning classes were often paternalistic and condescending and patronizing yet they were motivated by the spirit of noblesse oblige and assumed some responsibility for the physical, mental and moral health of those dependent on them. They anticipated in some measure the services provided today by the welfare state.

Chapter XL

I entered Whitelands College in September of 1936. The summer before was a time of anticipation and preparation, buying clothes and other equipment. My mother was as ignorant of what was required as I was, and as usual money was scarce. I well remember the feeling of loneliness and fear I experienced as I watched my trunk being loaded on the train for London, and said a tearful goodbye to my parents and sister.

The college had been established in the latter part of the 19th century by the Church of England to meet the demand for trained teachers necessitated by the 1870 Education Bill. It had been originally located in Chelsea but had moved into new quarters in Putney some years before I entered. The red brick buildings were attractively designed in a modified Byzantine style and were set in lovely grounds. The chapel was a prominent feature and public and lecture rooms were spacious and well furnished and equipped. The dining room, which had a dais and high table for staff and visitors at one end, contained some twenty tables, each seating ten girls, 5 seniors and 5 juniors, who were considered to be a "family" and always ate together. Our single rooms were very pleasant, furnished with divan beds and light oak built-ins. They were far superior to the Spartan dormitory accommodations my sons encountered when they entered their American Colleges.

The college offered a two year course to a student body of slightly under 200 women. Certain courses were mandatory – Principles and Practice of Education, Teaching Arithmetic, General English, Divinity and Health and Physical Education. Other subjects were by choice, though a balance had to be kept between academic subjects and artistic, musical and practical courses. Half of us chose training in Early Childhood Education, while the other half would teach in Junior/Senior Schools. At the end of two years we had to pass an examination to obtain the University of London Teaching Certificate.

Some of our courses were more interesting and valuable than

others, this largely determined by the ability and personality of the lecturer. I especially enjoyed history for Miss Muir was a fine historian totally dedicated to stimulating her students as individuals, while at the same time preparing them to teach history effectively.

The hardest and most dreaded part of college was practice teaching. Several times during our two years we were assigned to schools in London where we struggled to teach children who knew we were students under the watchful eyes of teachers who often resented us and those of our own critical lecturers. Practice teaching meant early rising, cold bus or train journeys, inadequate food, unco-operative children, unsympathetic adults and long evening hours of lesson preparation. The possibility of failure in this area hung over us like the sword of Damocles, for failure would mean no certificate and consequently no job.

My early months in college were marred by an unaccountable feeling of general malaise. Vague abdominal pains, variously diag-nosed as nerves, indigestion and homesickness erupted in March into acute appendicitis, necessitating a middle of the night operation in Putney Hospital. Two weeks there and four weeks convalescence at home put me far behind, but I managed to catch up sufficiently to avoid having to drop out for the rest of the year.

We attended morning chapel daily and the office of Compline was read at night though attendance was not obligatory. I was a member of the choir and we always sang the chants and psalms in plainsong, the opening verse sung in solo, the rest antiphonally. There were two very important festival days. One was October 21st, which was St. Ursula's Day, she being the patron saint of the college and the other was May Day. John Ruskin, Victorian man of letters, had instituted and endowed May Day ceremonies in the hope that Whitelanders, going out into the community as teachers would help perpetuate the ancient rites. We prepared a program of folk music and dances, there was a special chapel service but most important was the crowning of the May Queen. The girl chosen to fill this place of honour was elected by popular vote, generally on the basis of beauty, sweetness and goodness. Her gown was designed and made by students in the advanced needlework Department, she was crowned with and carried fresh flowers, wore a gold cross and headed a procession of May Queens of previous years.

We were allowed little freedom. Permission for late passes at weekends were hard to obtain and being late was regarded as a serious offence, leading to withdrawal of privileges. Our social life was mostly confined to weekend dances at our own and nearby colleges, where our partners were students from the men's colleges at Borough Road and St. Mark's and St. John's.

I made some very good friends at college. One, a fellow Moon-raker named Dorothy Atwell came from Devizes. We visited her in Swindon in 1954, but a few years later she died, leaving a husband and two boys. Winnie Barlow was very close and dear to me. We remain in touch and I have visited her several times at her home in Norfolk, getting to know her husband and daughters. Betty Glover from Ipswich had a distinguished career in education, is a fine artist and amateur actress. She has made three trips to the U.S., staying with us once in Glen Rock and twice in Chapel Hill.

We worked very hard in our second year in college. National events came and went without our noticing them much so wrapped up were we in our own concerns. However there was a lurking concern about the possibility of war, and though we had left college by the time the agreement at Munich was signed in September 1938, we all believed, along with Neville Chamberlain that it meant peace in our time.

Chapter XLI

Toward the end of my second year in college my father lost his job. His employer had become sick and the firm was reorganized and there was no place for him. It was a very anxious time and after much discussion, my father, by now in his middle fifties, decided to open his own business as a woodcraftsman. He created a small showroom in the front of our house and for the first time in his life began to experience some success. He got off to a slow start for he had a rather serious accident with an electric saw and cut his fingers very badly. He was sidelined for many weeks while his hand healed and two fingers on his left hand were permanently stiff. It was a difficult time for both my parents. Mother's heart was never in the business and she found the added work and change in lifestyle very hard to accept. In fact, she was never quite the same. I grieved for her but I also grieved for my father – his dream came true but it was only his – she never shared in it. However for the first time in their lives, money became relatively plentiful. After the initial lag the business took off and with the coming of the war and the arrival of the (comparatively) moneyed Americans, Father had more work than he could possibly handle. He worked long hours occasionally taking off to find timber. He always supplied people with tidbits of information, historical and otherwise to go with their trinkets carved and turned from local woods. So many orders poured in, that he could only fill a small part of them. He never refused an order, but he only executed those which interested him in a particular way. He had a few very satisfied customers but a host of exasperated ones, most of whom my poor mother was left to deal with. It was both sad and interesting that about this time certain characteristics especially in regard to money seemed to be exchanged from one to the other. My mother who had saved every penny during most of her life and had thus amassed a few hundred pounds now became very openhanded and generous, though in a controlled and orderly way, as indeed everything about her was controlled and orderly. My father, who had been generous to a fault when he had nothing, now became very conscious of money. For the first time in his life, he failed to turn over all his money to my mother and I think she was very hurt by this. As throughout the war her health began to fail she became oblivious and uncaring about this. She turned increasingly towards my sister and myself. My sister caused her some worry with her failure to find a job she liked and a series of unsatisfactory romances, but there was a closeness between them that was quite different from the relationship she had with me. I spent most of my school holidays with her – I was by then teaching in the Midlands – and she spent an occasional week with me. After my marriage, I spent a large portion of the two years prior to my departure for the United States with my parents, teaching in the local school and my time off was spent almost exclusively in my mother's company. When we were apart we enjoyed a rare exchange of letters. She wrote bi-weekly on Mondays and again on Wednesdays. Less than three months after I landed in New York on 10 February 1946 she was dead – after an operation which discovered the cancer which may have caused her deteriorating health for a good many years. Her death was the most shattering blow of my life. I had lost the comfort of her letters and the joy of answering them just at a time when I needed desperately to communicate with her.

My father and sister, who by this time was married, were equally desolate. Father struggled on, as best he could throwing himself more and more into his work, but he, of course, had lost his balance wheel and organiser when my mother went. He continued to make money becoming more and more parsimonious as time went on but he had a circle of friends who were good to him and to whom he could talk on a variety of subjects he found interesting and on which he was very knowledgeable. I am sure that the highlight of his last years was a six-month visit he made to the United States of America in 1949. He helped us move from a Long Island apartment to a small Cape Cod house in Glen Rock, New Jersey and enjoyed a visit to North Carolina where he became acquainted with David's parents and other relatives. He also enjoyed being a grandfather, my elder son David Gilmer being at that time a very enchanting though exhausting two-year-old. Father later developed diabetes ignoring his diet and overcompensating with insulin. After a long period of senility he died in Roundway Hospital, Devizes in June 1964 – a sad end to a man who I am quite sure had a largely unrealised potential for great brilliance. His death came as a relief to me and though I was fond of him and as a child was his close companion, as he had lost touch with reality so I had lost touch with him. A few years before his death my sister was found to have Hodgkin's disease which finally claimed her life. When my mother died May and I carried on a good correspondence for many years. Even after her illness disabled her, she was able to peck laboriously on a typewriter to produce a letter, though towards the end she could no longer do that. Again, I believe one of the highlights of her latter years was the visit she made to me in 1964. She was however ill while with me and I have always had an uncomfortable feeling that the journey was too much for her and precipitated the crisis.

We had a lovely time together talking over our childhood. I saw her several more times before her death and her condition was sad to see. I felt a sense of relief and release at her death too. My sister's husband outlived her by only six months, and she left two daughters, one married and one only fourteen. The fourteen year old went into a boarding school under the guardianship of her god-parents Jess and Ro Chandler. We went over to discuss these matters with them and one of the good things to come out of May's tragic family life was our wonderful friendship with this couple. Our last visits to Marlborough have been vastly augmented by knowing them and their family and it has been our great pleasure to entertain them here.

So except for my nieces, and some cousins I have no family left. I always visit my cousins in Wiltshire when we go to England – they have many mementoes of my grandmother Sharpe – and I have a cousin, a successful painter in Vancouver, B.C., Canada whom I have visited and with whom I exchange Christmas letters.

Chapter XLII

My years teaching in Birmingham were the least happy of my life. During my second year in college we were recruited for teaching jobs in all parts of the country. I had had a nice job offered to me in Seend, a pleasant village in Wiltshire, but Mother had been very insistent that I leave the country and try life in a big city. When the war broke out a year after I began teaching in Birmingham, the second largest city in England and centre of the automotive and small arms industry, Mother felt guilty that she had sent me into one of the danger areas. In fact, she worried about me a good deal of the time, that I would be bombed when in Birmingham and that I was having to bear a heavy responsibility of teaching Birmingham children in an evacuation area.

I knew no one in Birmingham though I had an aunt nearby whom I visited occasionally. I obtained lodgings or 'digs' as they were called in the vernacular, since on my monthly salary of twelve pounds, six shillings, ten pence a month (less than $50.00) I could not afford a flat of my own. For twenty-five shillings a week I had a room and my meals with the family, including a packed lunch which I took to school. I started work in September 1938, a year of hope that war would be averted and fear that it would not, and one that began with the fiasco of Munich and ended with the invasion of Poland and the declaration of war.

I was assigned to a Senior Mixed School in the northern part of Birmingham – a new school in a newly built area of modest semi-detached homes – an estate which housed people displaced by the vast slum clearance undertaken by many of Britain's large cities in the middle thirties. In spite of the gay little flowerbeds, what a dreary, drab, monotonous area it was after the age old charm of Marlborough. The boys and girls were for the most part children of factory and blue collar workers. They had failed to qualify for an academic secondary school and were working to complete their education by fourteen or fifteen, when most of them would predictably follow in their father's footsteps and work in the factories. It was quite a large school with each student year divided into five classes according to ability. The top streams were quite bright students and well motivated but the lower streams were poor scholastic material and had little desire to succeed. I was hired to teach English and history and was fortunate to work with the better students. The headmaster was a handsome urbane gentleman in his forties who was helpful and supportive, but on the staff there was an elderly spinster who had worked with him for many years and was his chief assistant. Woe betide the hapless young girl who smiled in the headmaster's direction or elicited any notice from him. There were three men on the staff who were worthy of mention. Two were ideal teachers personified – strong, just and respected by their students. They stood behind us young girls just out of college and made our lives bearable. The other was handsome in a devil may care insouciant way and with his bright blue eyes and toothbrush moustache, he looked rather like David Niven, the actor. He had travelled a good deal and had evidently come to the conclusion that teaching was a pretty easy way of making a living. He was married (unhappily) to an Australian girl he met during his travels. He was not averse to a flirtation with any of us who were foolish enough to encourage him. Lazy though he was, yet he could be a brilliant teacher, charming his students as he did women and possessed of the ability to bring the past alive and infuse his lessons with vitality. During the war, on evacuation duty in Leicestershire, he rocked both the Birmingham staff and the village by running off with the wife of one of the minor landowners in the area. He left his wife, she, her husband who was overseas fighting and also her two school-age children behind. I never learned what ultimately happened to them.

I was not happy in my first lodgings in Birmingham. While my landlady was a sweet, simple soul who spent much time bewailing the loss of a retarded baby daughter born to her very late in life, her husband was an ignorant bore – or boor – prototype of the American redneck. I detested him though my vividest memory of him now is that he always pronounced the name of Czechoslovakia's president Benes as 'Beans.' At the end of the first year I decided to look elsewhere for living quarters and after I returned from Abergavenny I lived with an elderly couple named Kendrick. They had a lovely house and rented a room to me only because they feared they would be forced to take in a soldier, refugee or some other homeless person. I could not have found nicer people – I really became the cherished daughter they never had. Childlessness seemed rather common in the generation before me. I think many women were unhappy because of it, feeling failures, but most of them seemed to sublimate their feelings by sharing the lives of their friends' children. There were several childless women in my life who gave me something of a mother's love and care in addition to that I received in such great measure from my own mother.

I was with the Kendricks during the terrible winter of 1940–41, sharing the Anderson shelter in the garden with them many a night from 6 p.m. to 6 a.m. until we felt Hitler would kill us with pneumonia if not with bombs. I stayed with them until a second evacuation plan was put into effect later on after Birmingham's water supply was badly damaged by bombs. Even then their home remained my base in Birmingham until in 1942 I left Birmingham and got a job in Loughborough, a Leicestershire town which was a larger version of Marlborough and where I had many friends. I corresponded with Mr. and Mrs. Kendrick till their death and had the pleasure in 1954, of taking my husband and two sons down to visit them in Worthing on the south coast where they had retired.

Chapter XLIII

The war was very hard on my mother. Just at a time in her life when money was becoming a little more available and May and I were launched in jobs which were acceptable and she was looking for a little easier life the war broke out with all its turmoil and worry and all the annoying and cumulative difficulties in daily living which it brought.

My father, on the other hand, while not happy was at least stimulated by it and caught up in war fever and the desire to play his small part in putting down Hitler. He was one of the few Englishmen who had been convinced for several years that a second war with Germany was coming. He harped on this theme to the point of being boring and/or laughed at and I sometimes felt as if Father and

Winston Churchill were the two lone voices crying in the wilderness. But in 1939 both were in the position to say "I told you so" – an unpopular but nevertheless self-satisfying state of affairs. Father was frustrated at being much too old for any type of war service. I think he felt cheated in the First World War by his near fatal attack of appendicitis followed by a long period of sub-normal health which kept him at home and now for the second war he was too old.

I had completed a year's teaching in Birmingham in July of 1939 and was home for the summer holidays when we were notified to return to our respective schools in late August. Plans for evacuation in case of war had been formulated during the previous year and we all knew roughly what the procedures would be. The ultimate decision whether to send a child away from home to the comparative safety of the country rested with the parents, but the government and education authorities did all they could to urge people to take advantage of the opportunities. After a frenetic distribution of gas masks and emergency rations, preparation of name tags, and assembly of luggage, we journeyed by train to Abergavenny, preceded by a harrowing and tearful farewell scene at the railway station. In Abergavenny, which is a small coalmining and marketing town in a lovely valley in South Wales, the children were housed in miners' cottages, farmers' homes and village and church halls. I myself was billeted in the home of the mayor of Abergavenny. It was outside a tiny stone miner's cottage, one of a row, on the afternoon of 3 September 1939, a perfect late summer day – what a lovely summer 1939 was – that I heard Neville Chamberlain's radio broadcast announcing that Britain was once again at war with Germany.

The first few months of war brought little change. For me, however, it was a hectic period of teaching children in unfamiliar surroundings with inadequate materials and accommodation and having to assume round the clock responsibility for our evacuees. But in the period of inactivity that came to be called the phony war most of the children trickled back to Birmingham and eventually their teachers were recalled and so in the winter of 1940-41 we were back in the city to bear the brunt of Hitler's bombing thrusts against Britain's industrial might.

Back in Marlborough, people were, as in Abergavenny, receiving evacuees from danger areas. In late August and early September 1939, a general exodus out of London had begun. School children were evacuated and other segments of the population such as blind and crippled people, expectant mothers and old people. Being seventy miles west of London and with a house on the main London to Bristol road, there was a constant stream of traffic past our door, vehicles laden with household goods ranging from mattresses to caged parrots. Many people were looking for accommodation and were prepared to pay any price. The most immediate problem that householders, including my mother, had to face was the making of black-out curtains for all windows. There was a run on material available and it was no easy matter to obtain it. The wardens would knock on the door at any chink of light and did not hesitate to levy fines. Torches or flashlights were also hard to come by and they were almost a necessity in the unlighted streets. There was some attempt at food hoarding by some people but rationing was instituted gradually and food shortages did not become apparent till later in the war.

The City of London School, a public school for boys, had chosen Marlborough as its evacuation site, sharing the educational facilities of Marlborough College while the boys were billeted in the town. One boy made his home with my parents. He was a good looking pleasant lad of sixteen but Mother found his care tiring and resented the intrusion on her privacy. He and my sister did not get along though he liked me on the rare occasions when I was home. In fact, I think he wished that either he was a few years older or I a few years younger. Towards the end of the war he was called up and wrote to my mother from Singapore. When last I heard of him he was a prosperous dentist.

Father's little business boomed during the war. As troops came into the town, so families and friends came to visit them. Many wanted souvenirs. By 1943 the Americans were coming in great force with much more spendable money than their British counterparts. But timber was becoming scarce and it was no longer possible in view of petrol rationing to scour the countryside in search of it. Yet, in spite of difficulties, Father remained busy one hundred per cent of his time and money began to come in very fast.

In 1940 after the fall of France, Father answered the call for able-bodied men too old for regular service to volunteer for home defence. Known first as the Local Defence Volunteers, later as the Home Guard, they helped erect and man pill-boxes, watched for enemy aircraft, parachutists and gliders, maintaining nightly vigilance. Poorly armed at first, some it was said had nothing but pikes, pitchforks and stout cudgels, they were eventually properly outfitted, but since the invasion of Britain was not attempted, they never had a chance to show their mettle. My father was a sergeant and took his responsibilities very seriously.

Chapter XLIV

The second evacuation from Birmingham early in 1941 took me to Leicestershire, a county to the north and east. I was in charge of a group of city children in a small village named Willoughby-on-the-Wolds and other groups of our pupils were billeted in villages nearby. The whole operation went smoothly – we had learned from our previous experience – and we soon became involved and integrated in village life. Our children were absorbed into the village school and although it was overcrowded we managed to teach as well as we could under the circumstances. I taught a class of eleven and twelve-year-olds who were part local children and part evacuees. There was a wide range of abilities and the differing environments of the pupils added interest as well as difficulties to my task. The headmistress was an elderly spinster, short and fat and very much of a martinet who took a dim view of the visiting children and an even dimmer one of any teacher who was young and reasonably attractive. But we came to terms and although I never liked her I had a sneaking admiration for the way in which she tackled a very difficult task, one she disliked, but always putting the education and welfare of both sets of children first.

Though it was a relief to be out of the city, out of the reach of any but a chance stray bomb and able to get an unbroken night's sleep, I very soon decided that I did not really like village life. There was too much gossip, too much busybodying and as a guest in an elderly farmer's house I was subjected to hours of tittle-tattle about people I did not know from the lady of the house – an eighty-year-old who was respected but also feared in the village. However, I had a lovely room there and better food than I had had in Birmingham where there were no extras to supplement our meager rations. Later I left there because of the farmer's illness and went to a small council house where I lived with a congenial couple with a small daughter. Though I involved myself in any village activities, such as whist drives and church bazaars, these were not very entertaining and in the winter the long dark evenings seemed endless. It was then that I took up embroidery as a hobby – it was Mrs. Kendrick in Birmingham who introduced me to it – and was soon doing very fine work. There was only one small shop in the village so every Saturday I caught a bus into Loughborough, the closest town, or into Nottingham or Leicester, big cities each about twenty miles away.

But I soon became part of a group of young people, the men, farmers who were exempt from military service, the girls, members of the Women's Land Army, teachers, or workers engaged in peripheral wartime occupations. We went to most of the village dances and got together at weekends. Sometimes the group was augmented by a young man home on leave and then it seemed the farmers got a little depressed because they felt out of the action and might be thought shirkers. Actually they worked long and hard to produce the food that was vital to Britain's survival. Somehow one or other always managed to find enough petrol for our expeditions. We had a good time but since we made no commitments, the relationships were easy and friendly and left us free to date others if we so desired. The farmer with whom I paired off was a well-built, handsome, blond young man who spent long hours managing a large farm for his uncle who was crippled with arthritis. He drove a very old car which had the habit of breaking down at inconvenient times. Our dating raised many eyebrows in the village and occasioned some gossip. But we managed to have a lot of fun together and for my part I was glad to be spared the war worry over dear ones that was the lot of so many of my friends.

Because I liked the area and the comparative safety from raids I applied for and obtained a job in Loughborough when recall to the city appeared inevitable. It was a wise move for I was back in a small town where life to me was preferable to that in either a big city or a small village. In fact, Loughborough, though considerably larger, was quite a lot like Marlborough in the life it had to offer. It was a market town with an attractive market square, and had an ancient church and some nice old buildings. It was the centre of a prosperous agricultural area and in addition was the site of several factories, among them the largest bell casting foundry in Europe. There was a college there which even in wartime offered some cultural opportunities. There was a pleasant residential area and here I obtained a room with a lady and her fifteen-year-old son. I was very happy living and working there, still seeing my old friends but making many new ones. I was teaching ten-year-old girls in a Church of England school and though the children were younger than any I had previously worked with I liked them and my colleagues. One of them, Barbara Partridge, became a close friend. She was a divorcee several years older, but she had a strong mothering instinct and she took me under her wing and did many nice things for and with me. She was a genius at concocting delicious food for the two of us out of the rations allowed and anything else she could obtain by fair means or foul. When we did our school all-night firewatching stint, she always produced bacon sandwiches for our supper. She had a bedsitting room in a house owned by a family named Taylor, who were later to become very dear to us. At the time I knew them then, their daughter Jean was an irrepressible teenager, but years later when she came out to Houston, Texas, to marry a man she had met in Edinburgh, David and I met her off the Queen Elizabeth in New York, hosted her for several days, then put her on a train to Texas. I recently visited her in Houston and her parents visited her several times and always stayed with us en route for Texas. Likewise, we stayed with them when we were in England. Barbara, my friend, had been in those Loughborough days, in charge of Jean some of the time, for Ian, a reserve air force officer recalled to duty, had crashed and received severe injuries and his accident necessitated Mildred's absence. Mildred and Ian are dead now but I remember them fondly as interesting, entertaining, charming people with a talent for making and keeping friends. Also my friend Barbara through whom I had of course met them, married again and moved with her husband to Trinidad and thence to the state of Washington, where I have seen her on two or three occasions when we have been on the west coast.

Another tie with Jean is in the person of Harriet Koch. She moved to Chapel Hill from Houston at the time we moved from New Jersey and Jean introduced us by letter. Harriet has become a dear friend and is in no small measure responsible for this book, encouraging me, nagging me and on the practical side doing the preliminary typing.

Chapter XLV

I was in Marlborough on summer vacation from Loughborough in August of 1943 when I met Lieutenant David Wharton of Greensboro, North Carolina. He had landed in Scotland aboard the troopship Queen Elizabeth just three weeks earlier. From Scotland his ordnance company had come down by train to Savernake Forest where ammunition was being stockpiled for the coming Normandy invasion. He himself, a Second Lieutenant, was billetted, along with a number of other officers in Tottenham House, an enormous bleak grey stone mansion – ancestral home of the Marquis of Ailesbury and deep in the heart of the forest.

My sister, who was very much involved in the Women's Voluntary Service, an organisation of women which looked after the welfare and entertainment of troops, persuaded me it was nothing less than my patriotic duty to attend a dance in the Town Hall on the evening of 5 August for British and American officers and sergeants. It took some persuading, as the few contacts I had had with the U.S. paratroopers stationed around Loughborough had not encouraged me to see more and so reluctantly I went along. Girls, of course, were in short supply and did not lack for partners or attention. David claims he first saw me in the bar having a drink with another officer, but back in the hall in the darkness of a spot dance, tall and goodlooking in his almost brand new uniform, he asked me for a dance. For the two weeks left of my time in Marlborough we met every night. When I returned to Loughborough daily letters arrived, we met in London and by great good fortune he was sent on a goodwill exchange to a British ordnance depot very near Loughborough. We became engaged at Christmas, buying my ring in London on 15 January. We were married in St. Mary's Church, Marlborough, 15 March 1944.

By that time I had had some correspondence with David's parents and sisters. David was the only son and middle child of William Gilmer and Annie McKnight Wharton, both members of long established highly respected families in Guilford County in North Carolina. At the time of our wedding his parents were residing in New York City. His parents were very proud when he was commissioned in the army and later were to follow enthusiastically his successful business career with Cone Mills, a Greensboro based textile company for whom Mr. Wharton had also worked. Strong Presbyterians, they expressed the hope that I was not a Catholic but otherwise they seemed willing and happy to accept an English daughter-in-law.

My parents, of course, had the advantage of getting to know David before our marriage. Like the Whartons, Mother had religion on her mind. As I related earlier she was relieved he was not 'chapel'. After our marriage, Mother said it was David's English sense of humour that endeared him to her, also his diffidence, modesty and lack of boasting, characteristics rarely found in Americans especially when on foreign soil. Though I feel sure it was a blow to Mother to know I would be living in America, after the war, she never expressed herself thus, though she told me on several occasions that she felt very proud to be sending a girl like me to America. She also said she was glad that I was the one going to live abroad rather than May, for she felt I had more resilience to withstand loneliness and homesickness and more personal resources on which to draw. That our marriage would be successful she never had any doubts, due in no small way, of course, to the assessment she formed of David's character and abilities.

Just like Winston Churchill said when he married Clementine Hoosier, I too can say "On 15 March 1944, I married David Wharton and lived happily ever after." Our wedding was small and followed by a reception at a restaurant in the High Street. We were married by Canon Swann, Rector of Marlborough, using the Church of England Order of Matrimony. I am afraid David thought the service interminable. Canon Swann was middle-aged, tall and ascetic looking with an autocratic, condescending manner. I think he must have disliked seeing so many English girls marry Americans for at a preliminary meeting he pressed David hard to tell him why he, a Presbyterian, wanted to be married in the Church of England. Finally David said, "Well, sir, I guess I just really want to marry Peg." Canon Swann laughed and said "Well, young man, at least you're honest" and after that he talked very kindly to us giving us the usual good advice. I had some reservations about choosing St. Mary's Church for my wedding. Though I had gone to St. Mary's Sunday School and to St. Mary's Girls' School and we had attended services there, albeit rather haphazardly, we were not in St. Mary's Parish but in Preshute Parish. I decided finally on St. Mary's because being in the town it was more accessible for outsiders than the little church two miles away. Now that my other family members are all buried in Preshute I still sometimes wish I could have the memory of being married in that tiny little church on the banks of the Kennet. However, St. Mary's is also a lovely church and after the service we had pictures taken in the fine old many arched Norman doorway with the chiselled dog tooth designs.

Our wedding was attended by most of our old friends though some were prevented by difficulties of wartime travel, and a group of American and British officers and other colleagues of David were present. His brother-in-law Walter Thayer, on wartime assignment in London, was our best man and his cousin Tom McKnight stationed at Tidworth was also there. My sister was my only attendant. Apart from the bride and groom, I think my father enjoyed the wedding more than anyone. As the father of the bride he enjoyed the speechmaking limelight at the reception and he was in his element. I remember his saying that he had always believed in the enterprise and derring-do of the Americans but did not expect to have it brought home quite so forcefully. Afterwards we drove to the station in a command car and caught a train to London and thence to Edinburgh for our honeymoon.

I returned to Loughborough to work out the necessary month's notice, after which I came to Wiltshire and lived in the forest, first in a small pleasant hotel and then we took a room in the gamekeeper's house. David was working fourteen to sixteen hours a day readying ammunition for D-Day (date at that time unknown) but we felt we wanted to be together as long and as often as we could. Finally 6 June arrived. David had gone to Cheltenham on a military errand and all day long I listened to planes going over. I knew it meant invasion and the beginning of the hardest fighting and the hope that it would herald the end of the war. A few days later David was transferred to Devon and I followed him and we had a pleasant interlude in Holsworthy staying at the White Hart Inn. But he was not there long. On 4 July, while I was attending Kathleen Burden's wedding in Potterne, he was on his way to France, his unit part of the great force keeping the front line troops supplied with ammunition. Apart from two or three brief leaves we did not meet again till I arrived in New York City, 10 February 1946, aboard the Queen Mary.

I returned home and after a brief stint of supply teaching in Bath, I obtained a job in St. Peter's Boys' School in Marlborough, where I remained till the end of 1945. I enjoyed my work there, made some good friends but most importantly was able to spend all my time when not at school with my parents, especially my mother, whose health was slowly deteriorating. In fact, I think my wedding day was the last time I remember Mother looking really well. Her malaise was very hard to pinpoint, she did not seem very ill but she certainly was not well, eating very little and growing thinner, paler and gradually weaker. The doctors prescribed tonics and rest and a visit for examination to St. George's Hospital in London uncovered nothing.

During those last months we found much to talk about – the conversation was no longer about the past but about my future – my hopes, aspirations and speculations. She shared my worries when I did not hear from my husband for long weeks at a time and my happiness when letters came. When he came on leave, Mother shared our joy. It was a happy time for Mother and me, though I think subconsciously we knew we were both waiting – I for the start of an exciting new life in another country and she for death and whatever may lie beyond. In late January of 1946 on a bitterly cold morning, we said our goodbyes without tears.

Chapter XLVI

My arrival in New York on 10 February 1946, was a cause of great excitement and the final attainment of a goal long hoped for. I had crossed on the Queen Mary which after long and distinguished service, both as a luxury liner and troopship, was making her maiden voyage as a transport for G.I. brides. The weather was rough most of the passage and the incidence of seasickness among the women, many of whom had one or two babies or small children, was so high that the ship's speed had to be reduced, lengthening the normal crossing time of five days to six. We embarked at Southampton sailing out of the Solent on a cold sunny day, the coast of England etched today as clearly in my mind as it was then in the crisp wintry air. Our stateroom accommodations were the wartime bunks of troops but the public rooms were lavishly furnished as in the pre-war years, and the Cunard staff fed us and looked after us well. We were warned en route that our husbands would not be at the pier to meet us but that we would be taken off the ship alphabetically in groups and bussed to a central location which proved to be the 7th Regiment Armory at Park Avenue and 66th Street. For many of the wives New York would only be an intermediate stop – they would go to their final destinations by plane or train, all travel arrangements being made and paid for by the United States Army.

The Sunday we docked, we were all on deck to see New York's celebrated Skyline and Miss Liberty lifting her lamp beside the Golden Door. In our threadbare wartime British 'utility' coats we shivered in the bitter wind and we were shocked to see chunks of ice floating in the river, in spite of a latitude more southerly than England's.

I was most surprised to look out from my vantage point high in the ship and see my husband far below though I found it hard to be certain of him partly because he was so distant and partly because I had never seen him in civilian clothes. But miraculously he spotted me and after indicating that I should remain where I was, he was at my side in a few minutes wearing the stevedore's badge which had gained him admission to the ship. Not at all sure of his right to be there we rather skulked around the back quarters of the ship for many hours waiting for the arrival of 'W' in the alphabetical sequence. But at last we – yes, he got on the bus too – were taken to the Armory where the final formalities were completed. It was five years to the day since he had been inducted into the New York 7th Regiment in that very building. We both took a short taxi ride to David's parents apartment at 242 East 72nd. Street. I remember the lovely livingroom, green carpeted with an oval coffee table on which stood a vase of deep red roses to welcome me. David's parents were in Florida at the time, whither they had gone because of his father's health. The next day I met Jane, his elder sister who lived a few streets away. Divorced, she lived with her small daughter and a nurse who looked after the child while Jane went to her job as a science teacher at the Brearley School. The following weekend we took the train to Albany to meet David's younger sister, Betsy and her family. Again I was impressed by the bitter biting cold the like of which I had never experienced in England. Very soon I went to Greensboro for the first time. David was on a business trip so we stayed at the King Cotton Hotel and I had a chance to meet his numerous aunts, uncles and cousins, all of whom were most welcoming. David's parents, consumed with curiosity, cut short their Florida stay and came back, not only to meet me but to get ready for their retirement.

The first weeks in the U.S.A. were hectic, crowded with new experiences. The most urgent task before us was to find an apartment we could afford, no easy task in the immediate post-war years. I was worried with the news from England of my mother's deteriorating health. Shortly after I left home she had entered Savernake Hospital and arrangements were made for an exploratory operation to be performed in the Radliffe Infirmary in Oxford. She died there in April after surgery disclosed inoperable cancer. It was impossible for me to return to England in time for her funeral. My one consolation was that she was spared further pain and the indignities of terminal illness.

Shortly after her death, we moved to our first apartment in Jamaica, Long Island. It was the second floor of a two-family house owned by an ex-G.I. and his English wife. In August 1947 on my thirtieth birthday my older son, David Gilmer was born. When he was two and while my father was visiting us we moved to Glen Rock, New Jersey, a small suburban town which was to be our home for twenty-eight years. Our second son Christopher John was born in 1950.

I felt somewhat less successful as a parent than in other areas of my life. I so wanted the best of my two worlds for my children that I fear I ended by giving them neither the brash self-confidence of the American child nor the sophisticated self-assurance of the English. However, both children proved to be intelligent, good students and relatively easy boys to raise. Today they are supporting themselves in interesting careers.

David graduated from Colgate University in 1969, became a professional photographer and is at present doing graduate work in his field in Austin at the University of Texas. He married Marianne Day in 1969 and they have two children, Samuel Day who is now 6 and Emily Margaret who will soon be 3. I see in David a strong resemblance to my father.

Chris joined the Peace corps when he graduated from Brown University in 1972. He spent three years in Thailand teaching English after which he became involved in refugee work in the Far East. He is employed by an international organization known as ICM (Intergovernmental Committee for Migration). After tours of duty in Bangkok, San Francisco and Kuala Lumpur, he now heads their office in Manila. He is married and has a small son, Benjamin David. We eagerly anticipate and enjoy his U.S. leaves.

My life in Glen Rock was a busy one with two children to raise and it became both busier and happier when I launched out into a resumption of my teaching career. My husband's business life brought us into contact with many interesting people and in the years we lived in Glen Rock, we made many friends. Our life there was rich and rewarding and was punctuated by many holidays both abroad and in the U.S.A. and in Canada. We made two exceptionally interesting trips to Thailand and the Far East, the first when Chris was a Peace Corps teacher in a high school in Buriram and a second in 1978 when he was an ICM officer in Bangkok and married to Suwanee Kanjana Akradet, a fellow teacher whom he had met in Buriram. We got to know her charming family and met many of his colleagues in Thailand, Singapore and Malaysia.

Now retired in Chapel Hill, we pursue a variety of interests some separate, some shared. We are able to travel, cement old friendships and make new ones. It is good to be nearer David's sisters and relatives and though we miss our sons for the first time in our lives, we can feel part of a large extended family. Truly life has been good to us.

Chapter XLVII

Making a permanent home in a foreign country is an ambivalent experience, especially for an adult not dissatisfied with her native land. It can comprise, to quote Dickens, the best of times and the worst of times.

When I arrived to live for some weeks in the heart of New York City, as one of the first English war brides, I was regarded as something of an oddity with my pronounced accent and typically English looks. Friends and relatives were very kind and hospitable, tradespeople were helpful, saving butter and other scarcities for one who, they believed, had been deprived of all luxeries and even some necessities for many years. I was interviewed by newspaper reporters both in New York and Greensboro, North Carolina, and was generally made much of. It was all quite exciting and gratifying but of course it was a short lived phase that already had begun to pall. I was then faced with the task of getting down to daily life in a strange country with little money to spend and many lonely hours to face.

My initial homesickness – or rather desire to return to England – was blunted by my mother's death – for I could not bear the thought of home without her. It was not until 1954 that we returned as a family and even then I went back with strong feelings of trepidation. But it was the first of many visits – all most enjoyable, but each time I have returned to America as to home. Any lingering feeling of wishing that I could live once more in England is dispelled by the knowledge that one can never go back. All I can do, like Wolfe's angel, is to look homeward. But I have built a new life in a new country by drawing on my experience and education in the old.

I wish I could count the number of times I have been asked "Do you like it here?" In fact I still sometimes get the question after nearly forty years of residence in the United States. To that fatuous query there is no one answer. Sometimes, yes, sometimes, no would perhaps be the most exact reply. The answer too might depend on one's mood and again there are many things one likes and many things which one does not. Any answer less than an enthusiastic affirmative would however raise the eyebrows of the inquirer, for of all people Americans appear to believe most strongly that theirs is God's own country and they have the most naive desire to be liked.

America is such a vast nation comprising people of many differing backgrounds, a country with such an enormous climatic and geographical range, that the changes of a successful adjustment by an English person are vastly increased if he settles in an area which bears some resemblance to England. I was fortunate to make my home in the Northeast in New Jersey within commuting distance of New York City, an area much like England and with a broader, less regional outlook than many other parts of the United States. It is this air of cosmopolitan life and thought, difficult to assess verbally, which I miss now that in retirement, we live in the South.

Americans are very proud – and rightly so – of their democracy and the personal freedom they enjoy. But other countries also enjoy the same freedoms and have democratic forms of government equally as efficient and effective as America's – a fact largely unrealised by many here.

I only voted once in England. Immediately after the war I cast a conservative ballot in the general election when Churchill was surprisingly defeated by socialist Clement Atlee. In 1952, recognising that in all likelihood I would spend the rest of my life in America, I became an American citizen, the final swearing in taking place in Hackensack, New Jersey. It was just in time for me to vote for Adlai Stevenson who in intelligence, oratory, and universality of thought seemed the American prototype of an English statesman. Ever since I have voted the straight Democratic ticket, for Republican conservatism, big business outlook and leanings toward isolationism hold no appeal for me.

There is no question that materially I have been much better off here than I would most likely have been had I remained in England. This modest material sufficiency has been due to hard work and successful careers for both of us and its attainment has contributed to my happiness. Another factor even more important is that I married into an upper middle class, cultured, well-educated family and it is from a similar class of people that we have drawn our many friends. Other friends are like myself of foreign birth for there is a camaraderie among people not born American.

I suppose when one has lived in two countries, life in neither is ever going to be completely satisfactory. One compares and contrasts constantly, usually to the detriment of whichever country one happens to be in at the given moment. I well remember at the time of the Suez Canal crisis in 1957, how pro-British my stand was in America, but how pro-American I became in England whither I had gone at a moment's notice because of my sister's illness.

One's need and longing for one's native country does not diminish with the passage of time. During the busy years of marriage, motherhood and career, nostalgia of necessity retreats into the background but now in the latter years early memories become sharper and the longing to visit again the haunts of youth is greater.

Though part of me will be forever English, I reflect that I have come close to having the best of both worlds and that I am one of the fortunate few who can call two countries home.

Chapter XLVIII

As I was growing up my mother was prone to reiterate her great good fortune at living in the time of history that she did. She firmly believed that never before in any lifespan had so many inventions come about to improve the lot of the common man. She would wax eloquent on the replacement of the horse as a means of locomotion, first by the railway, in the consistent growth and improvement of which she took much pride, and then by cars and buses. She rode a bicycle in her youth and could remember the penny farthing and the improved models which followed. She remarked on the superiority over the oil lamps of her childhood, first of gas and then electricity as the means of lighting houses and streets. She enjoyed the excellent mail service of pre-war England with its three or four daily deliveries, the first always arriving before breakfast. She appreciated its augmentation by telegraph and telephone, though she feared the former for the arrival of a telegram presaged bad news, and rarely used the latter as our circumstances were not sufficiently affluent to merit its installation. She appreciated the advantages of water, cold though it was in our house, drawn from an inside tap and the water closet adjoining our living quarters, over the outside water pump and earth closet down the garden path which were the facilities of her rural youth. She enjoyed the wireless tremendously and never ceased to marvel at music, plays, discussions brought into her very own livingroom for her pleasure and her children's edification. She only heard of television. Developed in England, its production was delayed by the war but she was eagerly anticipating it when death intervened. She liked "the pictures" too. Though she rarely went to a film during our childhood Mother and Dad went almost weekly to the local cinema in the High Street, a barn-like building now closed, in the last few years of her life. Her taste in movies was discriminating and she was quick to criticise the cheap and shoddy, detested Westerns but revelled in the good war films of the forties. In one of her letters to me in New York she wrote

> Dad and I went to see "The Three Caballeros" lást Saturday. It was surprisingly good. I don't usually like Walt Disney films but that one was out of the ordinary and I quite enjoyed it.

It was most likely the last film she saw and I couldn't have wished a better swan song for her. I remember very well her graphic description of her first visit to a moving picture show. She was in her early twenties and it was in Trowbridge, another Wiltshire market town. She spoke of girls and women fainting in the dark close atmosphere, their vertigo heightened by the intense flickering of the pictures and of some in the audience being so caught up in the screen action that they imagined themselves there and behaved accordingly. It was from her account a frightening experience.

Only of one modern invention did she feel that perhaps man had gone a bit too far and that was flying. Perhaps it was because we were located in the part of England where flying was pioneered and where many early accidents took place well nigh on our doorstep. Perhaps it was because of the lethal part played in the war by airoplanes. She was glad that I was able to make my journey to America by ship and did not have to resort to flying.

But apart from that never did she express any reservations about man's progress. She was, I think, glad of the expectation that her two daughters would make their lives in a world in which a great deal of the domestic drudgery of her early life had been eliminated.

My father, however, with his usual insight saw a little further and appeared to glimpse the perils of man's progress. He was sure that the world, if not in his lifetime, would eventually face racial problems, critical shortages and starvation because of overpopulation, overuse and abuse of resources, greed and ignorance. I do not know if my father had ever heard of Malthus but he was his true disciple.

Now some fifty years later, I in my sixties, reflect on how far I have passed my mother's expectations in the high living standard of middle class America. I have a plethora of labour saving devices which would stagger her imagination. But I also realize how much closer the whole world stands today to my father's dire prognostications. Much of the globe is facing now or will shortly face, mass starvation while we in America and in Western Europe live trapped in an extravagance of living from which there appears no easy escape. Our sporadic shortages of oil, steadily rising prices, inflation, political, social and labour unrest are all symptoms of a society that is over-using its raw materials, abusing its environment and is riddled by personal greed and corruption that may well preclude the hope that lies in retrenchment and self-sacrifice. Like my father I too tremble for the future of humanity, not for myself but for the young people who come after, those I have taught and those in our own family who are infants or as yet unborn.

But my world is so full of a number of things that interest me that I cannot spend time worrying about the future, more particularly when the individual is well nigh helpless to reverse or retard mankind's passage to destruction.

I awake each day to a sense of renewed purpose sometimes enjoying the daily round, the common task, sometimes facing a tomorrow that will lead me to fresh woods and pastures new. I love all aspects of life. I enjoy my husband's beautiful garden and its produce. I love my many lovely possessions, cooking the famous dishes of my native land, watching a watercolour composition develop under my brush, painting a special card for a particular friend. I enjoy my writing, my needlework, and knitting, sending and receiving letters, singing in the choir, playing bridge, making new friends and cementing ties with old – and most of all I am grateful for our happy marriage.

Each day I am thankful for health and strength and a sufficiency of funds – surely the three prerequisites for satisfaction in the years of retirement.

One of the favourite authors of my young womanhood was Winifred Holtby. Dying in her prime at the height of her literary excellence, she wrote on her deathbed "I have had a lovely life." Writing under happier circumstances I too can say "I have had a lovely life."